Student Voice

Turn Up the Volume
K–8 Activity Book

Russell J. Quaglia

Michael J. Corso

Julie Hellerstein

FOR INFORMATION:

Corwin
A SAGE Company
2455 Teller Road
Thousand Oaks, California 91320
(800) 233-9936
www.corwin.com

SAGE Publications Ltd.
1 Oliver's Yard
55 City Road
London EC1Y 1SP
United Kingdom

SAGE Publications India Pvt. Ltd.
B 1/I 1 Mohan Cooperative Industrial Area
Mathura Road, New Delhi 110 044
India

SAGE Publications Asia-Pacific Pte. Ltd.
3 Church Street
#10-04 Samsung Hub
Singapore 049483

Executive Editor: Arnis Burvikovs
Senior Associate Editor: Desirée A. Bartlett
Editorial Assistant: Andrew Olson
Production Editor: Melanie Birdsall
Copy Editor: Diane DiMura
Typesetter: C&M Digitals (P) Ltd.
Proofreader: Theresa Kay
Indexer: Karen Wiley
Cover Designer: Candice Harman
Marketing Manager: Lisa Lysne

Copyright © 2015 by Corwin

All rights reserved. When forms and sample documents are included, their use is authorized only by educators, local school sites, and/or noncommercial or nonprofit entities that have purchased the book. Except for that usage, no part of this book may be reproduced or utilized in any form or by any means, electronic or mechanical, including photocopying, recording, or by any information storage and retrieval system, without permission in writing from the publisher.

All trademarks depicted within this book, including trademarks appearing as part of a screenshot, figure, or other image, are included solely for the purpose of illustration and are the property of their respective holders. The use of the trademarks in no way indicates any relationship with, or endorsement by, the holders of said trademarks.

Printed in the United States of America

ISBN 978-1-4833-8278-4

This book is printed on acid-free paper.

15 16 17 18 19 10 9 8 7 6 5 4 3 2 1

PRAISE FOR STUDENT VOICE: TURN UP THE VOLUME K–8 ACTIVITY BOOK BY RUSSELL J. QUAGLIA, MICHAEL J. CORSO, AND JULIE HELLERSTEIN

This activity book will captivate your students through meaningful and exciting social building events. It will not be gathering dust in your resource collection. It will be one of the first you grab to develop excitement and the voice of your students. It puts fun in building life skills while meeting the ASCA standards.

—**Don Acker Sr.,** School Counselor

Engaging, insightful, and creative, this activity book provides rich tools through which students and teachers can learn about, practice, and apply the authors' principles in meaningful ways. Embedded with standards-based best practice strategies and a variety of technology applications, the activities offer an array of deeper learning experiences in a format that can be personalized for any classroom or group of students. *Turn Up the Volume* ensures a classroom environment in which student voice is valued and student aspirations are the focus.

—**Beth Havens,** Horry County Professional Development

This activity book is a teacher's dream! It is more than clear that the authors actually talked to teachers in the creation of this resource, which has it all: data-driven content, group discussions, engaging student activities, personal reflection and extension opportunities, connections to technology, AND designed for flexible use to meet the needs of individual teachers. Incredible, and a MUST-HAVE for every K–8 teacher!

—**Dr. Lisa L. Lande,** Executive Director of the Teacher Voice & Aspirations International Center

Teachers are not the only leaders in the classroom. Quaglia, Corso, and Hellerstein emphasize that any person who participates in the process of learning has a voice that should be engaged in schools. This book provides a plethora of opportunities for students to influence learning, take ownership, and develop a sense of worth and belonging in the classroom. Each activity was created and designed to guide students to be determined and goal oriented, while inspiring them to establish and work toward their future goals in school and life. This brilliant book showcases what seemed to be the impossible—a collaborative connection between students' active engagement and emotional involvement in their schoolwork, while linked to the Common Core Standards, 21st Century Skills, and International Society for Technology in Education (ISTE) requirements.

—**Tiffany Lewis,** First-Grade Teacher

The authors have once again designed an extraordinary road map for teachers to use in guiding students to find their true voice. A research-based road map, yes, but more important, a map teachers can use to guide students to find their voice through their experiences. The wonderful activities herein are inspiring, engaging, and interactive and ultimately lead students to discover their own unique voice and aspirations!

—**Rich McBride,** President and Executive Director, AESA

Partner the *Student Voice Activity Books* with the foundational book, *Student Voice: The Instrument of Change*, and the secret to turning schools and classrooms into vibrant communities of engaged learners will be revealed. Quaglia, Corso, and Hellerstein have masterfully woven together a practical and relevant fabric of activities that reinforces for students the importance of relationships, active and engaging teaching and learning, and exercising a sense of responsibility over one's own goals. Thanks to these authors, we now have a compendium of strategies designed to give students a meaningful voice in the educational process.

—**Dr. Raymond L. Smith,** Author of *School Improvement for the Next Generation* and *Evaluating Instructional Leadership*

One of the few books on education in the last several decades that has a touch of genius, this book gives teachers strategies that help them build and nurture relationships with their students and make learning more engaging and relevant to students' lives—resulting in higher levels of student achievement. The authors provide proven strategies and impart skills—connected to Common Core Standards, 21st Century, and ISTE requirements—that can be immediately applied to positively impact every student, teacher, and school leader in America.

—**Dr. Julie R. Smith,** Author of *Evaluating Instructional Leadership*

AVAILABLE FROM CORWIN
ISBN: 978-1-4833-5813-0

Contents

PREFACE: NO ORDINARY ACTIVITY BOOK ix
ACKNOWLEDGMENTS xvii
ABOUT THE AUTHORS xix

CHAPTER 1: BELONGING 1

Grades 6-8: Belonging Activities
- Pick a Number 3
- All About Me Cloud and Class Cloud 7
- Belong-Meme 9

Grades 3-5: Belonging Activities
- Personal Paper Doll 11
- Class Mascot 14
- The Who Are You? Interview 17

Grades K-2: Belonging Activities
- Alike and Different 20
- Buckets 22
- Cultural Connections 25

CHAPTER 2: HEROES 27

Grades 6-8: Heroes Activities
- I Can Be a Hero Poem 29
- Utilizing YOU! 31
- Gratitude 33

Grades 3-5: Heroes Activities
- Hero Traits 35
- Historic Museum Exhibit 37
- Tellagami About Heroes 39

Grades K-2: Heroes Activities
- My Everyday Super Hero Cartoon 43
- Hall of Fame 45
- We Can Be Heroes—Me and You 48

CHAPTER 3: SENSE OF ACCOMPLISHMENT — 51

Grades 6-8: Sense of Accomplishment Activities
- Marble Roll — 53
- Student Actions — 55
- Headline News — 59

Grades 3-5: Sense of Accomplishment Activities
- Award Show — 62
- How to . . . — 65
- Perseverance Phrase — 68

Grades K-2: Sense of Accomplishment Activities
- I Think I Can — 70
- Citizen Action Plan — 72
- Congratulations Card — 74

CHAPTER 4: FUN & EXCITEMENT — 76

Grades 6-8: Fun & Excitement Activities
- Heads Up! — 78
- Appy Hour — 80
- Un-Bored Games — 82

Grades 3-5: Fun & Excitement Activities
- Build a Band — 84
- Molding Minds — 86
- Story Starters — 88

Grades K-2: Fun & Excitement Activities
- Scenarios — 91
- Acting It Out — 94
- Digital Story Telling — 96

CHAPTER 5: CURIOSITY & CREATIVITY — 98

Grades 6-8: Curiosity & Creativity Activities
- Quick Question — 100
- The Curiosity Convention — 102
- Marshmallow Challenge — 104

Grades 3-5: Curiosity & Creativity Activities
- Genius Gallery — 106
- Mystery Picture — 108
- Invention Convention — 110

Grades K-2: Curiosity & Creativity Activities
- What's in the Bag? — 112
- Surroundings Scavenger Hunt — 114
- Mad Libs — 116

CHAPTER 6: SPIRIT OF ADVENTURE — 118

Grades 6-8: Spirit of Adventure Activities
- Student Speak — 120

Adventure Advice	122
Never Lose Sight of Your Goal	124

Grades 3-5: Spirit of Adventure Activities

Support Me Selfie	126
Adventure Action Cards	128
Bull's-Eye	130

Grades K-2: Spirit of Adventure Activities

Skills Within Reach	132
Oh, the Places You'll Go	134
Hands-On Goals	136

CHAPTER 7: LEADERSHIP & RESPONSIBILITY — 138

Grades 6-8: Leadership & Responsibility Activities

Tag Team Debate	140
Drawing Dictations	142
Values Auction	144

Grades 3-5: Leadership & Responsibility Activities

My Voice and Choice	147
Addressing Assumptions	149
Discuss and Decide	152

Grades K-2: Leadership & Responsibility Activities

Listening Blocks	156
What Do You Think?	158
Opportunity for Opinions	161

CHAPTER 8: CONFIDENCE TO TAKE ACTION — 163

Grades 6-8: Confidence to Take Action Activities

Time Capsule	165
Extreme Community Makeover	168
Letter to the Editor	170

Grades 3-5: Confidence to Take Action Activities

Confidence Commercials	172
Selfie-Confidence	174
Students Sharing Skills	176

Grades K-2: Confidence to Take Action Activities

Selfie-Confidence 2.0	178
Confident to Change	180
Career Quest	182

APPENDIX A: COMMON CORE STATE STANDARDS, GRADES K-8 — 184
APPENDIX B: PARTNERSHIP FOR 21ST CENTURY SKILLS, GRADES K-8 — 189
APPENDIX C: ISTE STANDARDS, GRADES K-8 — 190
INDEX — 192

To the students and staff who inspire and challenge us to always have high aspirations. You are constant reminders that there is no age requirement to improve the teaching and learning environment!

Preface:
No Ordinary Activity Book

You cannot always judge a book by its subtitle. Take this book, for instance. It is less about the activities, and more about the experience. It is intended to involve and inspire teachers and students. This book is both research- and need-based—designed to bring together sound practice with what teachers and students want and need to create an engaging learning environment that fosters students' aspirations.

The authors bring to this book critical professional knowledge, beliefs, and firsthand experiences in this field:

- extensive knowledge of over thirty years of research on student aspirations;
- involvement with teachers and students in Grades K–12 throughout the academic year, talking with and, most importantly, listening to them;
- belief that students have something to teach us and every interaction an opportunity to learn from students; and
- belief in a nonscripted approach to education, therefore never *telling* you what to do, rather, focusing on providing inspiring ideas for you to breathe life into.

You know your students best, not to mention they know themselves. Our goal is to provide a tool that you can utilize and adapt to meet the needs of your students. We hope and expect that you will integrate your professional knowledge with the knowledge of your students to bring this activity book alive.

Our background and beliefs are important, but this book is not just the result of our collective wisdom—it's the result of yours. We spoke with hundreds of teachers and asked them what they would value in an activity book. Their top ten wishes were to make sure that

- each activity is simple to implement, yet complex enough to keep students engaged;
- activities are age appropriate and can be used with groups of students with mixed abilities;
- activities are adaptive and can be personalized but are also generalizable;
- students can lead the activities;
- activities can be used in a wide range of contexts (in class and outside of school);

- activities do not cost money;
- activities can delve into "deeper learning" if teachers want to extend into richer investigations with students;
- activities are connected to our mandated curricula and standards;
- activities can be understood by parents or guardians at home; and
- activities are not a waste of my time or my students' time!

Tall orders indeed, but we asked because we wanted to know. We believe in the value of listening to, learning from, and responding to the teachers and students who are involved in the educational environment every day—those who inform and are directly impacted by the work we do.

What have we learned? That when activities are too complex, they become scripted rather than organic, and do not promote spontaneity or deeper learning. On the flip side, when activities are too simple, they become bland and unproductive. In response, we took great care to maintain flexibility in the activities, allowing for teachers to connect an individual's skill with the challenges presented. Did we get it right 100% of the time? Certainly not—that's an inherently impossible task. No two teachers, classrooms, or students are alike. Your expertise and knowledge of your students will allow you to create the experience that is right for your classes.

It's critical that when students work in groups, they still recognize their individual "print" on each activity, that no individual becomes camouflaged within the group. Therefore, we developed activities that involve the entire class while simultaneously meeting the individual student's needs.

Our work is based on the belief students have something to teach us. Thus, many of the activities do not have a defined ending. The ending should emerge with and be determined by each group. For example, some activities could take ten minutes, while others could take up to a week depending on how much deeper you want to take that specific learning. Each activity has an estimated time for completion, but again, it is not up to us to tell you how much or little time you should spend on any one activity. It is dependent on you, your students, and the circumstances of the moment.

It would also be naive for us to tell you what time of year to offer various activities. That is very personal and circumstantial. For example, in the beginning of the year, you may want to spend more time on Belonging activities; if you are working with a group of students who want to take their leadership to the next level, we would suggest the Confidence to Take Action activities; if the class seems flat, you should introduce activities driven by Spirit of Adventure or Fun & Excitement. The bottom line is that student groups will take activities to levels beyond what we imagined, while other activities will not have the desired impact on some groups. Throughout it all, please keep in mind—teachers are not the only leaders in the classroom. We suggest that students be provided opportunities to organize and implement the activities. This approach, in and of itself, will increase engagement in the classroom.

We promise this book is unlike any you have seen before. The activities are engaging, meaningful, and relevant to your students. They can be accomplished with virtually no financial implications, and while they are connected to school, they are not restricted to school. Each activity can stand alone and be implemented outside of the school setting. We made it a point to ensure that ALL activities are connected to Common Core State Standards (CCSS), 21st Century Skills, and International Society for Technology in Education (ISTE) requirements. Activities include personal reflections, group reflections, and extended learning opportunities. For Personal Reflection, have students select one or more of the prompts and write a journal entry, a poem, or song lyrics to share on a class blog or website. Use your own questions as well to generate a conversation about the activity. The Extended Learning sections are opportunities to continue the learning.

Why bring this all together in one book? We know it's important, and we know time is precious in schools . . . for students and teachers.

Alongside teachers' beliefs in taking the time to develop relationships and make learning engaging and relevant to students' lives, we realize teachers are accountable for ensuring a myriad of standards are met. They do this all on a fixed budget within a fixed amount of time. This book will not magically add hours to your day, but it is designed to help you maximize the time you do have with your students. All three authors have been teachers (and in multifaceted ways, still are). We know firsthand the challenges of the fixed resource of time. In and of themselves, these activities are a productive use of time. When done well, they will open up doors for extended learning, resulting in even more engaged learning in important content areas.

This book would not be complete if we did not ask students what is useful for them. We did. Not surprisingly, many responses were similar to those of their teachers. However, there were two distinct themes that were frequently echoed by students: *I want activities that are about ME!* and *The activities need to be fun.* Regardless of age—kindergarteners through seniors—students felt strongly that learning should be fun, with one student making an important distinction: "I want to be engaged, not entertained."

The feedback from students reinforced what we knew—that the activities need to be rooted in the very fabric of what guides our work each and every day: putting into practice the conditions that foster student aspirations. In order for teachers and students to work together in a manner where students' can realize their potential, the activities need to be grounded in research and a theoretical Aspirations Framework.

We define Aspirations as *the ability to dream and set goals for the future, while being inspired in the present to reach those dreams.* To understand, work toward, and achieve one's aspirations, there must be a future and present component. Aspirations are about *dreaming* of the future and *doing* in the present—combining the vision of what we want to achieve with the willingness to do what is necessary now to make that dream a reality.

In order to help schools and educators foster student aspirations, Drs. Quaglia and Corso have developed the Aspirations Profile, a visual model of behaviors that support and hinder success. The Aspirations Profile has two dimensions: Dreaming and Doing.

We can look at Aspirations graphically if we think of each aspect—present/doing and future/dreaming—as the X- and Y-axis of a grid.

ASPIRATIONS PROFILE

	Present/Doing Low	Present/Doing High
Future/Dreaming High	**Imagination**: Sets goals for the future but does not put forth the effort to reach those goals.	**Aspirations**: Sets goals for future and puts forth effort in the present to reach those goals.
Future/Dreaming Low	**Hibernation**: Has no goals for the future and puts no effort in the present.	**Perspiration**: Works hard in the present but has no goals for the future.

Source: Adapted from Quaglia and Corso, *Student Voice: The Instrument of Change* (2014).

Seen this way, the two aspects of the definition provide us with four categories:

Hibernation

Students in the Hibernation category do not think about the future, have no clear goals, and put forth no effort in daily life. Those in hibernation are stalled—they have neither a picture of where they want to go, nor the energy for doing much in the present. Such people lack a sense of purpose and rarely experience a sense of accomplishment in anything they do.

Perspiration

Perspiration is the category that describes someone who works exceptionally hard, always puts forth effort, but lacks direction or purpose. Such people are diligent but directionless; they are often busy but see no meaningful future in front of them.

Imagination

Students in the category of Imagination readily share their future plans but show little, if any, effort to reach those dreams. These individuals have positive attitudes about their prospects but take no steps in the present to achieve their goals.

Aspirations

Students with Aspirations are determined and goal oriented. With genuine aspirations comes the clear vision of a future destination and the passion for exerting oneself in the present to reach that destination. Such people have the ability to set goals for themselves and are inspired to work toward those goals *now*. They have a vision about what they want to do and who they want to become. They commit the energy, time, and resources required to meet their objectives.

The neat quadrants of the Aspirations Profile betray an obvious fact: Our aspirations operate on a dynamic continuum, more so than in a static set of boxes. Students may be in hibernation as they mindlessly recover in front of a television show after a long day at school, but that is not their permanent state. They may be in perspiration temporarily because you have given them an important task and they do not yet have a clear picture of how it fits in with their learning. A student who has been procrastinating on an assignment may fall into the imagination state, contemplating how nice it would be to get high praise for the work, knowing she has not put in the required effort. All students are not aspiring all the time. Yet, when they are, their full potential comes into focus. Students are not fully engaged when they are dozing or daydreaming or participating out of sheer duty. Students are revealing and realizing their full potential when they are taking action to bring about the goals they have set for themselves—a process of becoming who, not just what, they want to be.

The activities in this book are designed to guide students into the upper right quadrant of the Aspirations Profile, inspiring them in the present to establish and work toward their future goals—in school and life.

The Aspirations Profile unfolds in the Aspirations Framework, which outlines a way to recognize and develop students' aspirations. The Framework is based on Dr. Quaglia's 3 Guiding Principles that show up consistently in research and are at the core of what motivates students to achieve their dreams. We believe the 3 Guiding Principles must be present for students to have high aspirations.

GUIDING PRINCIPLES

The 3 Guiding Principles that support students' aspirations are:

Self-Worth

Self-Worth occurs when students know they are uniquely valued members of the school community; they have a person in their lives they can trust and learn from; and they believe they have the ability to achieve—academically, personally, and socially. With Self-Worth, students are more likely to persevere through difficult tasks and take the steps needed to reach their goals.

Engagement

Engagement occurs when students are deeply involved in the learning process as characterized by enthusiasm, a desire to learn new things, and a willingness to take positive, healthy steps toward the future. Students are meaningfully engaged when they are emotionally, intellectually, and behaviorally invested in learning. With Engagement, learning—and therefore participation in learning—becomes important in and of itself.

Purpose

Purpose exists when students take responsibility for *who* and *what* they want to become. Students need to explore what it means to have, and create, a successful and rewarding life. This is about more than deciding on a career. It is about becoming an involved, responsible member of the community and making choices that lead to a meaningful, productive, and rewarding life.

The Guiding Principles are lived out through 8 Conditions that emphasize relationships, active and engaging teaching and learning, and a sense of responsibility over one's own goals. We refer to these as the 8 Conditions That Make a Difference™ in our 2003 book, *Raising Student Aspirations: Eight Conditions That Make a Difference*.

8 CONDITIONS IN SCHOOL

Teachers create *Self-Worth* in the classroom when they foster these three Conditions:

Belonging: The belief that a student is a valued member of a community, while still allowing the student to maintain his or her uniqueness. By creating a sense of belonging, teachers foster students' self-confidence and investment in the community.

Heroes: The everyday people in students' lives who inspire them to excel and to make positive changes in attitudes and lifestyles. Teachers have prime opportunities to be Heroes to their students. Building relationships with students through support, guidance, and encouragement enables them to become more confident in their academic, personal, and social growth.

Sense of Accomplishment: The recognition of effort, perseverance, and citizenship—along with academic achievement—as signs of student success. When teachers take time to recognize and support students' efforts, it can help motivate them to persevere through challenges, creating an appreciation for hard work and dedication.

Teachers create *Engagement* for students when they are purposeful about creating lessons that instill the following Conditions:

Fun & Excitement: Students' active engagement and emotional involvement in their schoolwork. To foster Fun & Excitement in school, teachers can offer students new opportunities, as well as meaningful challenges, that are connected with their individual interests.

Curiosity & Creativity: Inquisitiveness, eagerness, a strong desire to learn and develop new or interesting things, and a longing to satisfy the mind with new discoveries. To sustain student motivation, teachers can devote extra attention to creating learning environments that promote questioning and creative exploration.

Spirit of Adventure: Students' ability to take on positive, healthy challenges at school and home, with family and friends. When teachers promote healthy decision making and healthy risk taking, students can become more confident and resilient.

Finally, teachers create a sense of *Purpose* for students by promoting the Conditions of:

Leadership & Responsibility: Students being able to express their ideas, make decisions, and show a willingness to be accountable for their actions. When teachers foster leadership, students become empowered to make just and appropriate decisions, take pride in their actions, and accept accountability for their choices.

Confidence to Take Action: The extent to which students believe in themselves and act in pursuit of their goals. Teachers can help build their students' Confidence to Take Action by having high expectations of students, providing support, and encouraging independent thinking.

The activities in the book are organized around the 3 Guiding Principles and the 8 Conditions that affect student aspirations. It would be naive of us, and misleading, if we claimed these activities would make your life "easier" as a teacher. We can promise, however, that they will add an important dimension to your teaching—one that enhances the learning environment for all by supporting the conditions that foster student aspirations. These activities are a venue through which students can use *their voice* to express themselves—their opinions, their values, their hopes and dreams. These activities promote a learning environment that is driven by interest, relevance, and engagement. As you and your students breathe your own life into these activities, connections will be made to the Common Core, and a dimension of realism will be added to 21st Century Skills. You will capitalize on technology, promote interdisciplinary connections, and engage students in practical, meaningful, and productive ways. (Maybe it does make your teaching life "easier" after all!)

Aspire ... Dream big. Act now. Commit to showing your students, and yourself, that this is unlike any other activity book you've seen before. These are not merely activities—they're experiences waiting to happen.

Acknowledgments

We would like to thank the most amazing team of people at the Quaglia Institute: Kristine Fox, Deb Young, Brian Connely, Susan Inman, Sarah Rawlings, and Sue Harper. Your unyielding dedication to student voice and aspirations is an inspiration to all. Your insights, support, and guidance are evident in this book.

PUBLISHER'S ACKNOWLEDGMENTS

Corwin gratefully acknowledges the contributions of the following reviewers:

Sandra Burvikovs, Teacher K–5
Gifted Specialist
Lake Zurich, IL

Erin P. Eckert, Principal
Donnelly Elementary School
Conklin, NY

Donna Eurich, Teacher
6th-Grade Language Arts
Renaissance Charter School at Cypress
West Palm Beach, FL

Marie Ortega, Educational Consultant
Verona, NJ

Joyce Sager, Teacher
Special Education Inclusion
Attalla, AL

Shawn White, Social Studies Chair
Weston McEwen High School
Athena, OR

Craig Yen, Teacher
5th Grade
Valle Verde Elementary
Walnut Creek, CA

About the Authors

Dr. Russell J. Quaglia is recognized globally as a pioneer in the field of education, known for his unwavering dedication to student aspirations and student voice. In addition to founding and leading the Quaglia Institute for Student Aspirations, he also founded and currently chairs the Aspirations Academies Trust, a sponsor of primary and secondary academies in the United Kingdom built upon his aspirations research. Most recently, he has founded and chairs the Teacher Voice and Aspirations International Center. Dr. Quaglia earned his bachelor's degree at Assumption College, a master of arts degree in economics from Boston College, and master of education and doctorate degrees from Columbia University, specializing in the area of organizational theory and behavior. He has been awarded numerous honorary doctorates in humanitarian services for his dedication to students. Dr. Quaglia's work has also led him to serve on national and international committees, reflecting his passion for ensuring that students' voices are always heard, honored, and acted upon. Follow Dr. Quaglia on Twitter @DrRussQ.

Dr. Michael J. Corso is the chief academic officer for the Quaglia Institute for Student Aspirations (QISA). He has a doctorate in education from Boston College, has been an educator for over thirty years, and has taught at every grade level kindergarten through graduate school. He is deeply committed to the belief that students are the agents of their own learning. This passion makes him a natural fit for work in the area of student aspirations. Dr. Corso has worked throughout his career to improve teaching and learning through teacher training and education. In his role at QISA, Dr. Corso combines research on student perceptions of their schools with educational theory and the living, breathing practice of students, teachers, and administrators. Follow Dr. Corso on Twitter @michaelcorso.

Julie Hellerstein is the director of student services for the Quaglia Institute for Student Aspirations (QISA). Ms. Hellerstein deeply believes that students and teachers must collaborate and partner to improve the school experience and increase learning in the classroom. She empowers her students to share their voice, ideas, and opinions. As director of student services, Julie plans and executes "Student Q-Team" workshops to increase student voice and aspirations at QISA's Demonstration Site schools. Ms. Hellerstein has hosted innovative student leadership conferences in Ohio, Idaho, and South Carolina. Prior to accepting a position at the Quaglia Institute, she taught social studies at Northmont High School in Clayton, Ohio, including *Link Crew*—a class in which junior and senior students are trained in helping new students transition to high school. Ms. Hellerstein was also part of a pilot program studying the utilization of the iPad in the classroom, which sparked her passion for engaging students with technology. Ms. Hellerstein graduated from the University of Dayton and is currently pursuing her master's degree in educational leadership. Follow Ms. Hellerstein on Twitter @hellerja.

CHAPTER 1

Belonging

> In physical education class, the teacher says, "We are going to learn how to do cartwheels. I need everyone who is right handed to stand to my right and everyone who is left handed stand to my left." In her class of twenty students, nineteen move to the teacher's right and one student moves to the teacher's left. The class giggles nervously and the lone student looks somewhat sheepish. Without missing a beat, the teacher stands next to the lefty and, looking across at the righties asks, "Now I need anyone who has learned how to do cartwheels before to switch sides." Five right-handers join the teacher and the lefty student. The teacher says, "Most of us are going to learn to do cartwheels starting with our dominant—the one we write with—hand. Those of you who are experienced cartwheelers have the challenge today of learning to do this with your nondominant hand. Let's begin."

A feeling of belonging is foundational to every student's experience of school. We define *Belonging* as being part of a group while still feeling accepted for who you are. Both halves of this definition are critical to genuine community. Mere going along to get along is not Belonging; nor, obviously, is going it alone. Each day of a young person's schooling, from the first day at preschool to the last day in high school, is shaped (or misshaped) by experiences with peers and adults that are either welcoming and friendly or isolating and alienating. Concerns over making new friends, fitting in, feeling accepted, and being liked are a part of each week and month and year. They are as important to young people in school as learning reading and math.

Given the importance of Belonging to the learning environment, educators have a responsibility to ensure that students feel safe, accepted, valued, and prepared to work together. It is difficult for a student to concentrate on an algebra assignment if he fears he will be bullied later that day. It is challenging for a student to ask a question in class if she is concerned her ignorance will be judged and laughed at. And it is nearly impossible for a student to do well on a test if he is afraid that getting an A will be met with ridicule among his less-than-academic in-crowd.

More positively, Belonging is characterized by experiences of accepting differences, of listening to one another's ideas with respect, of sharing common interests and goals, and of working together on joint projects. Such collaboration is one of the critical abilities called for by 21st Century Skills (see www.p21.org). But the community that underlies such a positive learning environment is not automatic; it must be achieved. Everyone must work together to ensure that acceptance and respect remain in place.

Critical to fostering Belonging is providing students with opportunities to get to know one another. Belonging is further developed when students learn to value the uniqueness of each person and see how diversity can make a group stronger. The following activities are designed to help you nurture Belonging among your students. Even students who seem to know one another or who have been together as a group for a long time should refresh their experiences and knowledge of one another. Belonging can ever grow and deepen.

Grades 6-8: Belonging Activities

Pick a Number

(30–40 MINUTES)

Belonging:

Feeling like you are part of a group while knowing you are special for who you are.

Objective:

Students will be able to ask their classmates questions and form positive relationships with their peers.

Materials:

List of questions for each group; number spinner available at http://www.classtools.net/random-name-picker/37_jk2H7U; Google form (optional).

> **Common Core:**
> Comprehension and Collaboration: CCSS.ELA-LITERACY.SL.6.1, 7.1, 8.1 Engage effectively in a range of collaborative discussions (one-on-one, in groups, and teacher-led) with diverse partners on grade 6, 7, 8 topics, texts, and issues, building on others' ideas and expressing their own clearly.
>
> **21st Century Skills:**
> Communication and Collaboration, Critical Thinking and Problem Solving
>
> **ISTE/NETS:**
> Creativity and innovation B

Steps:

- Instruct students to break up into groups of eight to ten. Give each group the list of questions on the next page. One person in the group will be assigned as the question asker but should answer a question, too.
- Have each student choose two numbers by spinning the random picker wheel. This number will correspond to a question on the next page.
- Each student will answer the two questions selected when he or she has spun the wheel. As a teacher, you should answer some questions, too.
- Have students share one number with the questioner who will read the question they have been assigned. After answering the first round of questions, the exercise should be repeated to answer the second question.

Questions

1. What is something you think that should be taught in school that currently isn't?
2. What Disney character would you want to be your best friend?
3. What is your favorite food?
4. If you could travel anywhere, where would it be?
5. If you could be an animal, which one would you be? Why?
6. What can you teach me?
7. What is your favorite sports team?
8. What chores do you have to do at home?
9. Do you have any pets? If not, what pet would you like to have?
10. When is school fun for you?
11. When are you at your most creative?
12. Who is your role model?
13. When do you take healthy risks at school? For example, try something even if you do not know if you will be good at it.
14. Describe the current state of your room. Is your room messy or clean?
15. Who do you think is the most successful person alive today? Explain.
16. What is your favorite school supply?
17. Do you have any nicknames? Who gave them to you?
18. What is the best book you have read?
19. What is your biggest win or success of the week?
20. Are you an early bird or a night owl?
21. What is your most challenging school subject?
22. What is your favorite childhood toy?
23. What talent would you really like to have?
24. Would you rather play in a pool or the snow?
25. What is your birthday?

26. What is your lucky or favorite number? Why?
27. Name a quote or song lyric that describes your life.
28. There is a movie being made about you. What actor or actress should play you?
29. What state do you think you should actually live in?
30. What is your favorite day of the week? Explain.
31. What is the best thing about going to this school?
32. What is your favorite lunch food?
33. What is one thing you would change about school?
34. How many siblings do you have? How many cousins?
35. What is your favorite TV show?
36. What is your favorite app?
37. What is the best thing someone has ever done for you?
38. What is your pet peeve? What annoys you?
39. Who has influenced you the most this past year?
40. What qualities make an effective teacher?
41. What is something nice that you have done for someone else?
42. What TV, book, or movie character is most like you?
43. What foreign country would you like to live in?
44. Describe one of your favorite school projects.
45. What is your favorite dessert?
46. What is your idea of the perfect weekend?
47. Who is your favorite musician?
48. What language would you like to learn?
49. Who is your role model?
50. What do you do in your spare time?

Copyright © 2015 by Corwin. All rights reserved. Reprinted from *Student Voice: Turn Up the Volume K–8 Activity Book* by Russell J. Quaglia, Michael J. Corso, and Julie Hellerstein. Thousand Oaks, CA: Corwin, www.corwin.com. Reproduction authorized only for the local school site or nonprofit organization that has purchased this book.

Personal Reflection:

Have students reflect on the activity and prepare ideas that they will share in the group activity.

- Ask: Why is it important for us to get to know each other? How does this impact your experience in this class? How does it impact your learning?
- Explain: Although we are all individuals, we also belong to one class. We need to respect each individual in our classroom community.
- Ask: How can we achieve this? What does a classroom community look like? What actions do students need to take?

Group Activity:

- As a class, come up with a class rule that all students agree to follow that reflects the importance of classroom community. Students must collaborate with each other and with the teacher to create this rule. Post the rule in your classroom and on the class website.

Extended Learning:

Option 1: Have students work in small groups to form their own questions. Play another time with student created questions. Or repeat with the questions provided by having students choose new numbers.

Option 2: Students will create a getting to know you questionnaire on Google forms or another simple quiz or survey creator tool. Have students partner up and answer each other's questions. For quiz tools go to http://www.teachthought.com/technology/35-digital-tools-create-simple-quizzes-collect-feedback-students/.

Notes:
_____
_____
_____
_____
_____
_____
_____

Grades 6-8: Belonging Activities

All About Me Cloud and Class Cloud

(ABOUT 50 MINUTES)

Belonging:
Feeling like you are part of a group while knowing you are special for who you are.

Objective:
Students will be able to create a personalized word cloud and contribute to a collaborative class word cloud. Students will be able to identify similarities and predict trends.

Materials:
Access to computers; Wordsalad or another word cloud generator (available at http://www.educatorstechnology.com/2013/09/6-great-apps-to-create-word-clouds-on.html); Edmodo, or class blog (extended learning).

> **Common Core:**
> CCSS.ELA-LITERACY.W. 6.6, 7.6, 8.6 Use technology, including the Internet, to produce and publish writing and link to and cite sources, as well as to interact and collaborate with others, including linking to and citing sources.
>
> **21st Century Skills:**
> Communication and Collaboration, Information, Communications and Technology Literacy
>
> **ISTE/NETS:**
> Creativity and innovation A, B, D

Steps:
- Have students brainstorm a list of words including their interests, future goals, and personality characteristics.
- Direct them to the Wordsalad app. This tool generates a "word cloud" from text that students provide. Students will edit the shape, the direction of the words, and the colors to personalize their world clouds.
- To start, students will click the plus sign in the corner and begin building their cloud. Students will enter words and click start. Next, students can edit the format. Students can export their images to save or share.
- Next, ask students to generate a list of words to describe the class as a group. Tell them to get creative. Have them define the goals, attributes, and personality of your class. Everyone should contribute to a list.
- Then create a class word cloud using all the students' input. One student can be the scribe for the class.
- Before printing or posting the word cloud, have students predict what the common trends in this word cloud will be. The trending words will appear larger in the word cloud.

Source: Created using Wordsalad.

Personal Reflection:

Have students choose three words in their personal word clouds and reflect on why they picked these words.

- Ask: What do these words mean to you? Suggest that in their explanation, they include links to relevant websites for classmates to learn more about their interests, values, or personal characteristics. Share this on a class Edmodo page, social media page, or class blog.

Group Discussion:

Why is it important to acknowledge and embrace both similarities and differences?

Extended Learning:

Option 1: Have students post their word clouds to Edmodo, a class blog, or class Twitter account.

Option 2: Have students help you create a bulletin board in your classroom displaying the word clouds.

Notes:

_____
_____
_____
_____
_____
_____
_____
_____

Grades 6-8: Belonging Activities

Belong-Meme

(ABOUT 50 MINUTES)

Belonging:

Feeling like you are part of a group while knowing you are special for who you are. Your uniqueness and individuality are what make you a special and important part of the school. It is important for you to feel a sense of Belonging in order to be truly who you are and who you want to be.

Objective:

Students will be able to create an Internet meme based off research that promotes the Condition of Belonging.

Materials:

Internet, device or computer; photo-editing software or app (example: Meme Something). Modify to use markers and posters, if technology is not available.

Steps:

Instruct students to research ways to increase belonging, respect, or acceptance in middle schools or middle school classrooms. Based on their research, have students pick a topic related to Belonging on which to focus. For example, students can research the effectiveness of mix-it-up lunch days, or anti-bullying strategies.

Students should then apply their knowledge to create an Internet meme that supports their topic.

- Students should analyze popular Internet memes and look for patterns. What characteristics do they share? Students should create a meme with their audience in mind.

- Students should decide who their audience is. Is it teachers? Principals? Their classmates? Younger students? Students of all ages?

Common Core:
CCSS.ELA-LITERACY.CCRA.W.4 Produce clear and coherent writing in which the development, organization, and style are appropriate to task, purpose, and audience.

CCSS.ELA-LITERACY.CCRA.W.6 Use technology, including the Internet, to produce and publish writing and to interact and collaborate with others.

21st Century Skills:
Communication and Collaboration, Information, Communications and Technology Literacy

ISTE/NETS:
Creativity and innovation A, B, C, D

Communication and collaboration A, B, C, D

Research and Fluency A, B, C, D

Critical Thinking, problem solving, and decision making A, B, C, D

Digital citizenship B

Technology operations and concepts A, D

- Next, students can brainstorm ideas for their new meme. Students will pick the visual for their meme by searching the Web, taking their own original photographs, creating an original graphic design, or drawing a picture. Students can also come up with creative tag lines that will catch their audiences' attention.
- Using Meme Something, have students select a photo from their gallery or take a new photograph. Then, write a creative text line.
- Next, have students decide what information they want to go along with the meme when they post it online. They may consider posting a question, a relevant quote, a surprising statistic, or Web links to informative resource pages. Check out the My Voice National Report for some relevant information (www.qisa.org).
- Have students upload and share their meme on their own social networks and other online communities.

Source: Photo by Julie Hellerstein.

Personal Reflection:

- What did you learn from this assignment?
- How much awareness were you able to generate?
- What kind of feedback did you receive from peers or your target audience?

Group Discussion:

Have students share their post with the class and explain their related relevant research. Invite other students to ask relevant questions about their purpose, research, and meme.

Extended Learning:

Have students track the retweets, regrams, or likes on their memes. Use a free trial of social media software like sproutsocial.com or hootsuite.com. What content received the most feedback? What kind of feedback did it receive?

Notes:
_____
_____

Grades 3-5: Belonging Activities

Personal Paper Doll

(40–50 MINUTES)

Belonging:

Feeling like you are part of a group while knowing you are special for who you are. Your uniqueness and individuality are what make you a special and important part of the school. It is important for you to feel a sense of Belonging in order to be truly who you are and who you want to be.

Objective:

Students will be able to express their interests, values, beliefs, and hobbies coherently to their classmates through a visual display and oral presentation.

Materials:

Headshot of each student in the class, cardstock, magazines, glue, scissors. It is best to laminate the paper doll once students are finished to prevent wear and tear.

Option: Students may use an image-editing app or program to make a digital paper doll like Dibu's Monster Maker app or Pickle's Paper Dolls (extended learning) app.

Steps:

- Ask students to cut out their head from their printed picture and glue it on cardstock template. You may want to do this step depending on the ability of students.
- Instruct students to decorate the body by making a picture collage with cutouts from magazines. Students should include pictures of their hopes and dreams, current interests, and their values.
- Tell students to prepare to tell their classmates about three different pictures on the doll's body that are especially meaningful to them.

> **Common Core:**
> CCSS.ELA-LITERACY.SL.4.4
> Report on a topic or text, tell a story, or recount an experience in an organized manner, using appropriate facts and relevant, descriptive details to support main ideas or themes; speak clearly at an understandable pace.
>
> CCSS.ELA-LITERACY.CCRA.SL.4
> Present information, findings, and supporting evidence such that listeners can follow the line of reasoning and the organization, development, and style are appropriate to task, purpose, and audience.
>
> CCSS.ELA-LITERACY.CCRA.SL.5
> Make strategic use of digital media and visual displays of data to express information and enhance understanding of presentations.
>
> **21st Century Skills:**
> Creativity and Innovation
>
> **ISTE/NETS:**
> Communication and collaboration B
> Creativity and innovation

Personal Reflection:

- How did creating the paper doll help celebrate what makes you special?
- Were any of the paper dolls exactly alike? Why?
- Explain how your classmates are unique.

Group Discussion:

Invite students to individually present their paper dolls. Students should introduce themselves and explain the importance of three different pictures on their doll's body. The audience can raise hands and ask the student who is presenting a getting-to-know-you question based on his or her doll.

Extended Learning:

Using the ShowMe app, have students create a digital media presentation. Students will take a picture of their paper doll. Next, they will record a voice-over describing the paper doll. Students can use the marker feature to draw arrows to point out three different pictures on their doll's body that represents their interests and hopes and dreams.

Students can create a paper doll-like monster by using Dibu's Monster Maker app.

Students who are interested in paper dolls can use Pickle's Paper Doll app to select outfits for six different girls from different cultures.

Notes:

_____
_____
_____
_____
_____
_____
_____

Grades 3-5: Belonging Activities

Class Mascot

(40–50 MINUTES)

Common Core:
CCSS.ELA-LITERACY.SL.4.1
Engage effectively in a range of collaborative discussions (one-on-one, in groups, and teacher-led) with diverse partners on *grade 4 topics and texts*, building on others' ideas and expressing their own clearly.

CCSS.ELA-LITERACY.SL.4.4
Report on a topic or text, tell a story, or recount an experience in an organized manner, using appropriate facts and relevant, descriptive details to support main ideas or themes; speak clearly at an understandable pace.
Production and Distribution of Writing.

CCSS.ELA-LITERACY.W.4.4
Produce clear and coherent writing in which the development and organization are appropriate to task, purpose, and audience.

21st Century Skills:
Critical Thinking and Problem Solving

ISTE/NETS:
Critical thinking and problem solving A

Belonging:

Feeling like you are part of a group while knowing you are special for who you are. Your uniqueness and individuality are what make you a special and important part of the school. It is important for you to feel a sense of Belonging in order to be truly who you are and who you want to be.

Objective:

Students will be able to collaborate with peers to define the values and key characteristics of the class. Students will be able to personify a class mascot.

Materials:

Purchase an animal beanie baby or other small stuffed animal that will serve as your class mascot all year; social media account of your choice (extended learning).

Steps:

Before the class mascot arrives, have students brainstorm words that represent their class. What do they believe is important? How should students treat each other and act?

- **Name the mascot:** Have students write down a name and an explanation of why the name would be a good choice. Collect the ideas and have students vote. Encourage students to pick a name that represents the personality of their class.
- **Pick a birthday for the mascot.**
- **Poem:** Beanie Babies have heart shaped tags that contain a short poem about the stuffed animal. Have the class create a new poem and write it on a new tag for the beanie baby. The poem should represent what the class believes in. Refer to the students' brainstorm list for content ideas.

Source: Photos by Julie Hellerstein.

- **Meet the Class Mascot:** Invite students to write letters to the new mascot welcoming him or her to the class. Students should include important information about what it means to be in the class and any personal information about themselves as individuals—like their hopes and dreams, favorite food, favorite hobbies, family members, favorite color, and so on.
    - Compile these letters into a binder to begin your class mascot journal.
    - Have students read their letters out loud while they hold the class mascot.
    - Encourage students to be active listeners and ask questions.
- **Take a Picture:** Once everyone has presented, take a class picture with your new mascot.
- **Include the mascot** in the majority of your classroom activities such as sitting on the carpet during read out louds, during review games, during lunchtime. Have him or her join you as an important member of your classroom community.

Personal Reflection:

Have students reflect on why is it important to share about themselves to others. Why is it important to listen to others about who they are?

Group Discussion:

Ask students: How did this activity help us to get to know each other better? How did this activity help us bond as a group? Do you think our class mascot feels welcomed? Explain: How should we welcome new students? How should we welcome students we do not know as well to make them feel important? Why is it important to share about yourself and what you like?

Extended Learning:

Continue to use your class mascot to increase the Condition of Belonging. Foster Curiosity & Creativity by using the mascot in writing activities. Visit http://www.scholastic.com/teachers/top-teaching/2013/04/engaging-young-writers-home-class-mascot-writing-project for directions.

As a class, create a social media account for the class mascot. The class mascot account can share pictures, updates, and give shout outs to students!

Option: Have students adopt a free Webkinz pet on Webkinz World at http://www.webkinz.com and play virtual games.

Notes:

Grades 3-5: Belonging Activities

The Who Are You? Interview

(ABOUT 50 MINUTES)

Belonging:

Feeling like you are part of a group while knowing you are special for who you are. An important part of fostering Belonging is learning about each other. This activity uses student interviews as a way to learn about each other.

Objective:

Students will be able to communicate with peers by asking questions, listening, and speaking.

Materials:

"All About Me" worksheet, pencil; podcast tools, iMovie, or TouchCast app (extended learning).

Steps:

- Have students fill out an "All About Me" worksheet. Then, collect them.
- Begin by asking students to talk about what it means to interview someone. Have students think of reasons why people interview others. Ask students to draw on their experiences. What interviews have they seen before? What made it interesting? Sometimes interviews are interesting because both the interviewer and interviewee are passionate about the topic. Sometimes interviews are interesting because the interviewer is learning something new and unique about the person being interviewed.
- Tell students that interviewers do their research and come prepared with written questions. They avoid questions that could be answered with a yes or a no. Many news reporters create open-ended questions that lead to more questions, depending on what the person says. Give examples and practice these kinds of questions.

Common Core:
CCSS.ELA-LITERACY.SL.4.1
Engage effectively in a range of collaborative discussions (one-on-one, in groups, and teacher-led) with diverse partners on *grade 4 topics and texts*, building on others' ideas and expressing their own clearly.

CCSS.ELA-LITERACY.SL.4.4
Report on a topic or text, tell a story, or recount an experience in an organized manner, using appropriate facts and relevant, descriptive details to support main ideas or themes; speak clearly at an understandable pace.

CCSS.ELA-LITERACY.W.4.4
Produce clear and coherent writing in which the development and organization are appropriate to task, purpose, and audience.

21st Century Skills:
Social and Cross-Cultural Interaction, Collaboration, Communication, ICT Literacy

ISTE/NETS:
Digital citizenship B

Technology operations and concepts B

Research and information fluency A

Communication and collaboration B

CHAPTER 1: BELONGING

- Pair students with a classmate they do not know well. Hand each student the "All About Me" worksheet about the student they are interviewing. Ask students to notice what they have in common with their partner and what is unique, special, or different. Have students mark on the paper. Instruct students to make a circle next to what they have in common with their partner and a star next to an answer that is different.
- Based on the worksheet, have students form two new open-ended questions: One question will be about something they noticed they have in common (circle), and one question will be about something that they noticed is different or unique (star).
- Have students get with their partner. Student A will start and ask his first question about something they have in common. Student B will respond. Student A should carefully listen to Student B. Student A can ask a follow-up question if something sparks his or her attention to keep the conversation going. Then, have the students switch roles.
- Next, have students take turns asking their question about something that is unique. Follow the same procedure.

Personal Reflection:

Ask students to reflect on what they liked most about this experience. What was most difficult?

Group Discussion:

Discuss: Even though we are all different, we have a lot in common. Each student's uniqueness creates a great class. Asking questions is a great way to learn about others.

- Why is it important to talk about things we have in common?
- How was this experience interesting to you? Was it easy to come up with a follow-up question? Why is it important to talk about things that make us different?
- Why was this interesting to you? Did you learn something new? What did you learn about your partner?

Extended Learning:

Students can research and watch popular interviews. What kinds of questions are asked? Another enrichment opportunity might be to record each student interview and create a podcast.

Create an iMovie by using the news reporter theme music and picture lay out or use the TouchCast app.

Read "How to Conduct an Interview" article at http://www.scholastic.com/teachers/lesson-plan/how-conduct-interview.

All About Me Worksheet

Name:

Birthday:

Have you ever moved before?

Hobbies and activities:

Describe your family:

Do you have any pets?

What is your dream job?

What are you doing right now to help you achieve your dream?

What you look for in a friend:

What was the last book you read?

What accomplishments are you proud of?

Who was your teacher last year?

What do you want to learn more about?

Favorite school project:

Favorite song:

Favorite school subject:

Favorite food:

Favorite animal:

Favorite movie:

Favorite season:

Copyright © 2015 by Corwin. All rights reserved. Reprinted from *Student Voice: Turn Up the Volume K–8 Activity Book* by Russell J. Quaglia, Michael J. Corso, and Julie Hellerstein. Thousand Oaks, CA: Corwin, www.corwin.com. Reproduction authorized only for the local school site or nonprofit organization that has purchased this book.

Grades K-2: Belonging Activities

Alike and Different

(ABOUT 50 MINUTES)

Common Core:
CCSS.ELA-LITERACY.SL.K,1,2.1 Participate in collaborative conversations with diverse partners about kindergarten, *grade 1, or grade 2 topics and texts* with peers and adults in small and larger groups.

21st Century Skills:
Social and Cross-Cultural Interaction, Communication, Collaboration

ISTE/NETS:
Communication and collaboration B

Belonging:
Feeling like you are part of a group while knowing you are special for who you are. An important part of fostering Belonging is for students to understand each other and celebrate what makes them special.

Objective:
Students will be able to write or draw what makes them special and see how they are important to the class community.

Physical Activity:

- Explain to students that they are going to play a game that will be a fun way to learn more about their classmates. We will learn ways we are alike and ways we are different and unique.
- Have students form a big circle. Tell them they will need to listen carefully and take a big step into the circle when you say a sentence that describes them. If it doesn't describe them, then they will stay in their original spots.
- Begin with something simple: Step forward if you are wearing socks today. Allow time for students to look around and see the different groups. Ask students to return to their original spot.
- Continue calling different characteristics that highlight similarities and differences.
    - Step forward if you have brown eyes.
    - Step forward if you have a brother.
    - Step forward if you have pets.
    - Step forward if you like to color.
    - Step forward if you like to play outside.
    - Step forward if you like to play basketball.
    - Step forward if you are a student in _____ class!
    - Step forward if you go to _____ Elementary School.

Be sure to add your own.

- Next, tell students they will continue learning about each other by making a class link chain of our talents and interests.

Materials:

Colored strips of paper, markers, tape.

Steps:

- Give each student five strips of colored paper.
- Ask each student to write or draw something that is special about him or her on a strip of paper, for example, I can count. I love dogs. I am a big brother.
- Once all the strips are complete, put the chain together and have the students hold the chain.
- Next, discuss the individual links and some of the interesting information.
- When the chain is finished, hang it in the classroom for the students to see!

Personal Reflection:

Invite students to reflect on the following questions:

- What are some of your talents, interests, and skills?
- How are your talents similar to and different from those of other students?

Group Discussion:

Share with the students how all people are special in many different ways. Indicate the many talents right in this classroom. Ask: What did you learn about a friend today?

Extended Learning:

Watch and share a relevant YouTube video clip, or TEDTalks for Kids with family, classmates, and others. Select an age-appropriate online article, song, or book that relates to Belonging or similarities and differences.

Check out "It's Okay To Feel Different" lesson plan from Teaching Tolerance at http://www.tolerance.org/supplement/its-okay-feel-different-primary-grades-k-2.

Check out "Everyone's a Helper" lesson plan from Teaching Tolerance at http://www.tolerance.org/supplement/everyone-s-helper-primary-grades.

Grades K-2: Belonging Activities

Buckets

(ABOUT 40 MINUTES)

Common Core:
CCSS.ELA-LITERACY.RL.K.1
With prompting and support, ask and answer questions about key details in a text.
CCSS.ELA-LITERACY.RL.K.2
With prompting and support, retell familiar stories, including key details.
CCSS.ELA-LITERACY.RL.K.3
With prompting and support, identify characters, settings, and major events in a story.
CCSS.ELA-LITERACY.RL.K.10
Actively engage in group reading activities with purpose and understanding.
CCSS.ELA-LITERACY.RL.1.1
Ask and answer questions about key details in a text.
CCSS.ELA-LITERACY.RL.1.2
Retell stories, including key details, and demonstrate understanding of their central message or lesson.
CCSS.ELA-LITERACY.RL.1.3
Describe characters, settings, and major events in a story, using key details.
CCSS.ELA-LITERACY.RL.2.2
Recount stories, including fables and folktales from diverse cultures, and determine their central message, lesson, or moral.

Belonging:

Feeling like you are part of a group while knowing you are special for who you are. Students can make a difference through daily kindness and being accepting of others.

Objective:

Students will be able to express how their words and actions impact others and themselves.

Materials:

Have You Filled a Bucket Today? A Guide to Daily Happiness for Kids by Carol McCloud, buckets for each student, pom-poms, MEME Something app (extended learning).

Steps:

- Read the book *Have You Filled a Bucket Today? A Guide to Daily Happiness for Kids* by Carol McCloud.
- Tell students that you believe they can all be bucket fillers. Have them raise their right hand and say the bucket pledge: "I (say your name) pledge to be a bucket filler."
- Check for comprehension. Ask students to recall key information from the book. Does everyone carry an invisible bucket? What is the bucket filled with? What types of actions does a bucket filler do? What happens if you are a bucket dipper? Can you fill your own bucket by emptying someone else's bucket? Is it important to reflect and think about your own actions and say I am going to be a bucket filler today?
- As a class, create a list of bucket-filler action steps for students to help the classroom community and school community. For example, help a classmate read, introduce yourself to a new student, ask someone different to play at recess, or sit with someone new and share classroom materials.

- Give each student his or her own real bucket. (White, paper paint buckets are available in most home hardware stores. Ask the art teacher for help and see if the store will make a donation.) Have students decorate the buckets with their names and anything else that represents them.
- Hang the buckets in the classroom with students' name on them. A clear, plastic hanging shoe rack works well.
- Fill another bucket with small pom-poms.
- Explain the procedure: When a student fills a classmate's invisible bucket, both the bucket filler and the classmate will get pom-poms added to their buckets. You may decide students will put in the pom-poms based on the honor system. You may decide to create a small form for students to fill out to describe the action and then review it and fill the pom-poms yourself. This is up to you based on your preference for accountability. You may also want to designate time on a regular basis to share bucket-filling stories and examples. Giving specific, genuine praise will help students understand positive behavior better.
- Once a students' bucket is filled up, the student will get a sticker on their bucket. It is important to explain to the students there is no prize for filling the bucket up the most times because filling up your bucket already makes you feel good!

> **21st Century Skills:**
> Initiative and Self-Direction, Leadership and Responsibility, Communication
>
> **ISTE/NETS:**
> Creativity and innovation C

Personal Reflection:

Have students create a Bucket Book. Students can write or draw about how full their bucket is and give reasoning every day.

Group Discussion:

Have students stand up when you read a statement that matches what bucket fillers would do or put their head down on the desk if the statement refers to bucket dipper. Have students reset to a normal sitting position after each statement.

- Tell a classmate that you don't like his picture.
- Follow the rules.
- Open the door for someone.
- Give your teacher a mean look.
- Help pick up a mess.
- Invite a new friend to sit with you at lunch.
- Take a friend who is hurt to go see the school nurse.
- Help a friend learn a new game at recess.
- Ask someone in class to read with you.
- When you see someone crying, ask if they are okay.
- Tell your classmate to go away.
- Not letting someone play with you.

- Push someone out of the way.
- Cut in front of someone in line.
- Draw a friend a picture.

Ask: How does being a bucket filler help create Belonging in our classroom?

Extended Learning:

Have students create an Internet meme (using the Meme Something app) about how they filled someone's bucket or how someone filled their bucket. Students can take a picture of their bucket or another picture and enter text.

Create a bucket filler video using iMovie or another movie-making app. Students can share stories about how they felt after they did something nice for someone. Share with other classrooms.

Obtain free Bucket Filler Resources online at http://www.bucketfillers101.com/free-resources.php or check out Pinterest for other ideas!

Source: Photo by Julie Hellerstein.

Notes:
___
___
___
___
___
___
___
___

Grades K-2: Belonging Activities

Cultural Connections

(40–50 MINUTES)

Belonging:

Feeling like you are part of a group while knowing you are special for who you are.

Objective:

Students will be able to identify similarities among peers with diverse backgrounds.

Materials:

Book: *Same, Same But Different* by Jenny Sue Kostecki, Google form (optional), Skype (for extended learning).

Steps:

- Read *Same, Same But Different* by Jenny Sue Kostecki.
- Have students recall details of the story by answering questions with prompting.
- What kinds of questions did the two characters ask each other?
- How were Kailash and Elliot the same?
- How were Kailash and Elliot different?
- What was the message of the story? Can you be friends with someone who is different?
- How did the students connect with each other? How did they communicate?
- As a class, brainstorm questions that you could ask someone to get to know them better.
- Make a collaborative document with a list of questions.
- Brainstorm ways to celebrate similarities and differences.

Common Core:
CCSS.ELA-LITERACY.RL.K.1 With prompting and support, ask and answer questions about key details in a text.
CCSS.ELA-LITERACY.RL.K.2 With prompting and support, retell familiar stories, including key details.
CCSS.ELA-LITERACY.RL.K.3 With prompting and support, identify characters, settings, and major events in a story.
CCSS.ELA-LITERACY.RL.K.10 Actively engage in group reading activities with purpose and understanding.
CCSS.ELA-LITERACY.RL.1.1 Ask and answer questions about key details in a text.
CCSS.ELA-LITERACY.RL.1.2 Retell stories, including key details, and demonstrate understanding of their central message or lesson.
CCSS.ELA-LITERACY.RL.1.3 Describe characters, settings, and major events in a story, using key details.
CCSS.ELA-LITERACY.RL.2.2 Recount stories, including fables and folktales from diverse cultures, and determine their central message, lesson, or moral.

- Create an opportunity for your students to have a pen pal from a different classroom, school, city, state, or country. Use the list of student-created questions as a resource.

Personal Reflection:

Invite students to think about how Kailash and Elliot celebrated their similarities and differences. Then ask them to describe a similarity they have with a peer. Have them think about and share one difference they have with a friend.

Group Reflection:

Have students collaborate to form a long list of getting-to-know-you questions that will uncover both similarities and differences among students. Students can formulate questions on a Google form or tech tool of their choice. Encourage students to ask each other questions from the list throughout the year. Students can add to the question list when they think of a good getting-to-know-you question. Having a long list of conversation starters for students will promote Belonging in your classroom. Discuss: How will getting to know each other better help us feel like we belong?

Extended Learning:

Set up a *Mystery Skype* to connect with other classes around the world! Students will ask each other questions via Skype to figure out the other students' location. Students can interact and ask different questions to see similarities and differences in action. Be sure to assign each student a different role to keep students engaged with a certain task. See https://education.skype.com/mysteryskype/how-it-works#nav for further information.

21st Century Skills:
Social and Cross-Cultural Interaction, Communication, Collaboration, ICT Literacy

ISTE/NETS:
Communication and collaboration A, B, C

Source: © michaeljung/Thinkstock Photos

Notes:
___
___
___

CHAPTER 2

Heroes

> Once a week, the Lunch Buddies Program pairs willing older students with younger students who have special needs to share a meal together. Typically the special needs students eat in their self-contained classroom. The experience of eating together benefits all students by developing mutual respect and support. Students enjoy one another's company and learn how to interact with those who are different. The school sees the Lunch Buddies program as among the best learning experiences it has to offer.

Having a Hero—a role model, mentor, teacher, or any trusted other—is critical to a student's success at school. Numerous studies point out the importance of such positive relationships to students' academic, social, and personal well-being. Students tell us all the time that they work harder for teachers they believe care about and respect them and will actually withhold work from teachers they believe do not.

Once younger students are over the idea that Batman and Wonder Woman are Heroes, and once older students are over the idea that Tom Brady and Serena Williams are Heroes, they share that the everyday Heroes in their lives, the people that make a difference are their parents, their teachers, their friends, and people in the community like police officers and firefighters. While it may make some educators uncomfortable to be thought of as Heroes, this is what students say. There is no escaping the fact that second only to parents, teachers are among the most influential people any of us encounter in the course of a lifetime. Check this against your own experience: Consider the number of teachers that have had an influence on your life.

The characteristics that young people identify in the people they consider Heroes are obvious ones like attention, respect, concern, and care. But there are also less obvious ones like having high expectations and holding them accountable for their actions and schoolwork. It is not just the "nice" teachers that are accounted Heroes by students, but the ones who will not let them get away with things, who "call us on our stuff," and who make clear what the boundaries and expectations are.

In addition to the adults in a school being Heroes to students, students can be Heroes to one another. Whether a student finds care and kindness among her peer group and friends, or whether older students encourage and mentor younger students, all students can learn to play this supportive role for one another. The following activities will guide you to help students recognize the everyday Heroes among them and help you teach them how to be Heroes to one another.

Grades 6-8: Heroes Activities

I Can Be a Hero Poem

(30–40 MINUTES)

Heroes:

Having people who believe in you and are there for you when you need them. The condition of Heroes is about helping students recognize that they are Heroes to the people they interact with every day. Heroes do not have to be adults.

Objective:

Students will reflect and identify what they have to offer and their potential to be an everyday Hero at school and in the community through writing a poem.

Materials:

Paper, writing supplies; iPad or other device with The Poetry App (Josephine Hart).

> **Common Core:**
> CCSS.ELA-LITERACY.W.7.4
> Produce clear and coherent writing in which the development, organization, and style are appropriate to task, purpose, and audience.
>
> CCSS.ELA-LITERACY.CCRA.W.6
> Use technology, including the Internet, to produce and publish writing and to interact and collaborate with others.
>
> **21st Century Skills:**
> Creativity and Innovation
>
> **ISTE/NETS:**
> Creativity and innovation B

Steps:

- Have each student write a personal poem.
- Invite students to start each line of their poem with "I am . . ."
- Students should include statements that identify their hopes, background, skills, and personal attributes. This may include favorite quotes, family traditions, customs, for example.
- Suggest that the end of the poem be "Because I am all of these things I can be a Hero."
- As the teacher, write your poem first and share with the class.
- Discuss with students that we all have so much potential to be a Hero because we are so unique.
- Allow students to write several drafts of the poem.
- Next, students should type their poems under the My Poems of The Poetry App. Click the plus sign in the corner to begin. Students will create a title for the poem and then tap on the text to start composing the poem. Students can increase their vocabulary by tapping the "inspire me" button. Next, students will read their poem by pressing the red, recording button.

Personal Reflection:

- What does it feel like to be a Hero?
- What can you do today to be a Hero to someone at school?
- What can you do to develop the condition of Heroes for yourself?

Group Reflection:

- How do you see students being Heroes at your school?
- Why do you think it is important for students to respect each other?

Extended Learning:

Search CNN for the online video *Heroes Young Wonder: Joshua Williams*. Watch and reflect. How did Joshua use his passion to make a difference? Explore the CNN Heroes website to read more heroes' stories and watch their videos.

Notes:
___
___
___
___
___
___
___
___
___
___

Grades 6-8: Heroes Activities

Utilizing YOU!

(40–50 MINUTES)

Heroes:

Having people who believe in you and are there for you when you need them. The condition of Heroes is about helping students recognize that they are Heroes to the people they interact with every day. Heroes do not have to be adults.

Objective:

Students will be able to research and report information on a charitable organization. Students will be able to evaluate how they can utilize their own skills and talents to give back to the community. Students will be able to collaborate with peers to form a unique charitable action utilizing peers' talents and skills.

Materials:

Sticky notes, whiteboard, notecards, markers; devices or computers for research; Blogger (extended learning).

> **Common Core:**
> CCSS.ELA-LITERACY.RI.7.1
> Cite several pieces of textual evidence to support analysis of what the text says explicitly as well as inferences drawn from the text.
>
> CCSS.ELA-LITERACY.CCRA.R.7
> Integrate and evaluate content presented in diverse media and formats, including visually and quantitatively, as well as in words.
>
> **21st Century Skills:**
> Communication, Collaboration
>
> **ISTE/NETS:**
> Research and information fluency A, B
>
> Creativity and innovation A, B
>
> Communication and collaboration A, B, D

Steps:

- Tell students they are going to create a *K-W-L* chart (what I **K**now, what I **W**ant to know, what I **L**earned) about charitable giving or philanthropy. Write the letters *K*, *W*, and *L* on the board as column headers.

- Give students sticky notes.

- Explain that the *K* column will have information about what they know about charitable giving and philanthropy. Have students write about charities they know and provide examples of when they have done a charitable act on sticky notes. Have them place the notes on the board under the letter *K*. Review as a class before proceeding.

- Next, students will write down what they want to know about charitable organizations— questions about charitable acts, philanthropies, or charities that they might want to get involved with. Have students place these questions in the *W* column.

- Next, have students research a charity of their choice. They should write down three different pieces of information they learned about that charity on sticky notes. These should be placed in the *L* column.
- Review the chart as a whole class.
- Divide the class into small groups of five to seven students.
- Hand each student a notecard and markers. Ask all group members to write down something they are good at doing or really enjoy doing.
- Have the groups read over their group's collection of talents.
- The groups should now brainstorm what kind of charitable act or organization the group could support together using everyone's unique talents. How would each talent be put into action? Have students name their charity and a description of everyone's role.
- Each group should share with the class.

Personal Reflection:

- Are you using your talents to serve others? How?
- Come up with three action steps that you can do that would help you be an everyday Hero to others.
- What was the most interesting thing you learned about a charity with researching?
- What was the most interesting talent you learned that a classmate had?

Group Reflection:

- Why is it important to utilize everyone's individual talents?
- How can we use everyone's individual talents to make a difference in our classroom?
- Why are charitable acts important?
- How does participating in charitable acts make you feel?

Extended Learning:

Have students pick a charitable act that they researched or they came up with, plan, and execute the action. Students can share their plan on blogger.com, a blogging dashboard through Google.

Notes:
_____
_____
_____

Grades 6-8: Heroes Activities

Gratitude

(20–30 MINUTES)

Heroes:

Having people who believe in you and are there for you when you need them. Often when students think of Heroes, they talk about famous athletes or celebrities. However, there are everyday people who make a difference in our lives by talking to us and listening to us.

Objective:

Students will be able to recognize the everyday Heroes in their lives. Students will be able to produce clear and coherent writing to thank a Hero.

Materials:

Thank you cards or computers with access to http://www.punchbowl.com/ecards/thank-you?gclid=CJjxg7KpncECFYMF7Aodu3oALg.

> **Common Core:**
> CCSS.ELA-LITERACY.CCRA.W.4 Produce clear and coherent writing in which the development, organization, and style are appropriate to task, purpose, and audience.
>
> CCSS.ELA-LITERACY.CCRA.W.6 Use technology, including the Internet, to produce and publish writing and to interact and collaborate with others.
>
> **21st Century Skills:**
> Communication and Collaboration, Leadership and Responsibility
>
> **ISTE/NETS:**
> Creativity and innovation B
> Digital literacy

Steps:

- Ask students to think of a teacher, coach, neighbor, or staff member who really believes in them.
- Allow students to share stories or anecdotes.
- Next, instruct students to write a thank-you note or card of appreciation to a person who made a difference in their life. Students can create a handwritten card or a free, digital card using punchbowl.com.
- For the digital card, have students Google punch bowl free thank you notes and select a template. Students will edit and design the front, inside, and the envelope and postage to send to their Hero.
- Students should give specific reasons and identify the characteristics of the person that makes them their Hero.
- Once the cards are complete, encourage students to send the card.

Personal Reflection:

- Who is your most important everyday Hero right now? Explain.
- Who do you think you are a Hero to and why?

Group Reflection:

Besides writing thank-you cards, what else could we do to show our gratitude to people who are everyday Heroes to us? Make a list on the board of creative ways to say thank you.

Next, brainstorm ways to build relationships or get to know other staff members or adults in your life.

- Interview your principal.
- Invite a teacher to eat lunch with you and your friends.
- Pick out one adult at school you would like to get to know better and talk to them once a week during your free time.
- Take the time to get to know the school custodians, lunch workers, secretaries, and other support staff.

Extended Learning:

Share your gratitude 2.0!

- Create an iMovie trailer using superhero format to recognize a role model. Focus on the characteristics you admire about this role model.
- Nominate your Hero at the Foundation for a Better Life site.
- Using an app such as Red Stamp, create and send a personalized thank you note to your everyday Hero.
- Tweet about your Hero!
- Create an Instagram post about your Hero. Select a picture of you and your Hero, a quote that reminds you of your Hero, or even a selfie of your Hero. Explain why this person makes a difference to you!
- Create a YouTube video about your Hero!
- If your teacher has a website or a class blog, ask if you can post your writing there! Blogger is an easy blog tool.

Notes:

Grades 3-5: Heroes Activities

Hero Traits

(30–40 MINUTES)

Heroes:
Heroes are people who care about each other and support each other just as friends do every day. This activity encourages students to recognize themselves and their friends as Heroes.

Objective:
Students will be able to identify and spell grade-appropriate words that describe a Hero by consulting references. Students will be able to match word appropriately with a classmate.

Materials:
Brown paper bags, slips of paper, writing supplies.

Steps:
- Discuss: What makes your friends or classmates special? What does it mean to be a good friend?
- Have students brainstorm a list of characteristics and positive traits that their friends have. Students should give examples of specific actions.
- Next, have students list adjectives that describe a good friend or everyday Hero.
- Invite students to add to the list by using synonyms. Students may use a dictionary, vocabulary book, thesaurus, or the Internet for help.
- Give each student a brown paper bag. On the outside of the bag, ask students to draw a picture of one way they personally help others. Create your own paper bag, too.
- Give each student several slips of paper.
- Explain to students that they will be filling each classmate's bag with positive feedback. For example, "Riley is a good listener." "Hunter sat with me at lunch when I was a new student." "Destiny always helps me with my homework."
- Have students sit in a circle; you should join students in the circle. Facilitate the activity by having students pass their bag to their right. Students should write down a characteristic, word, trait, or comment or draw a picture about their peers' description of how they help others. Alternatively, they may write a positive memory about the student.

Common Core:
CCSS.ELA-LITERACY.L.4.2.D
Spell grade-appropriate words correctly, consulting references as needed.

CCSS.ELA-LITERACY.L.4.4.C
Consult reference materials (e.g., dictionaries, glossaries, thesauruses), both print and digital, to find the pronunciation and determine or clarify the precise meaning of key words and phrases.

21st Century Skills:
Communication, Leadership and Responsibility, Social and Cross-Cultural Interaction

ISTE/NETS:
Digital citizenship B

- Have the students pass their bags again, and again until everyone receives their own paper bag back filled with slips of paper about them and the way they help people.
- Allow students time to read and reflect on all the positive traits they have.

Personal Reflection:
- What does it feel like to be recognized as a good friend or everyday Hero?
- What Hero quality do you want to develop?
- Can everyone be a Hero? Explain.

Group Reflection:
Can everyone be a Hero? Explain why or why not.

Extended Learning:
Create a Heroes dictionary using the word list that the class created to describe a good friend or Hero. Have each student pick a word. Students will write the definition, pick an illustration, and use the word in a sentence. Compile entries into a class book.

Option: Have students make multimedia pages and compile entries to create an iBook. Download iBooks Author free from the Mac App Store: https://www.apple.com/ibooks-author.

Notes:

Grades 3-5: Heroes Activities

Historic Museum Exhibit

(3–4 DAYS, INCLUDING PRESENTATIONS/WAX MUSEUM)

Heroes:
Having people who believe in you and are there for you when you need them.

Objective:
Students will be able to identify a historic Hero that demonstrates good character and research that person's life and accomplishments. Students will be able to integrate information on a person from multiple texts to produce a well-organized visual and audio presentation.

Materials:
Devices, computers, or books to research; ShowMe App; costumes.

Steps:

- Invite each student to pick a Hero in history. You may decide to create a list for students to choose from to better fit your curriculum.
- Have students research their Hero's accomplishments, traits, and characteristics. Students should find multiple nonfiction, informative texts to read about their Hero including a first- and secondhand account.
- Students should create a biography of their Hero. Include
  - a description of their Hero's accomplishments
  - a story about their Hero that shows their character
  - three facts about their Hero
  - a list of words to describe their Hero
- Next, explain to your students that you will be having a living Historic Heroes Museum exhibit. Have students take their research and rewrite it into a first-person speech. Students will record their voices and add visuals to create a video that can be played on a device at the Historic Hero Museum. This can be done through the ShowMe app or another tech tool of your choice. They will dress like their Hero and stand still during the museum event as if they were an actual wax statue!

Common Core:
CCSS.ELA-LITERACY.RI.4.9 Integrate information from two texts on the same topic in order to write or speak about the subject knowledgeably.

CCSS.ELA-LITERACY.RI.4.6 Compare and contrast a firsthand and secondhand account of the same event or topic; describe the differences in focus and the information provided.

21st Century Skills:
Creativity and Innovation, Communication, Initiative and Self-Direction

ISTE/NETS:
Creativity and innovation A, B, Communication and collaboration A Research and information fluency B, C

Source: Created using ShowMe.

- Plan back-to-back dates for the Historic Heroes Museum. Be sure to inform parents and the community of the event. Divide the class to present on two different days. One day half the class will be presenters and the other half will be museum attendees.
- Each student will dress up like his or her Hero. Students will have the participants hit play on the device and they will listen to the presentation.
- Have each student make a name tag to wear of his or her Hero.
- Set up the exhibits. Make sure each Hero is standing in a different spot in the room. Have students in small groups rotate through and visit each Hero, starting at different points. Students who are the attendees should write down one key fact about each person on a notecard or on their device.
- Allow wax characters to come alive and answer any questions and then have them quickly go back to being a wax statue.

Personal Reflection:

- What surprising information did you learn about your historic Hero?
- What characteristic do you share with your historic Hero?
- How does your historic Hero inspire you?

Group Reflection:

Compare historic Heroes. What did the Heroes have in common? What made them unique and special?

Extended Learning:

Invite other classes to walk through your museum exhibit.

Record the museum exhibit experience and create a documentary video with exclusive interviews with the historic characters.

Have another museum exhibit. However, this time have students interview and research their everyday Hero. For example, students can dress up like their coaches, nurse, babysitter, or teacher.

Grades 3-5: Heroes Activities

Tellagami About Heroes

(30–40 MINUTES)

Heroes:
Having people who Believe in you and are there for you when you need them.

Objective:
Students will be able to think critically and formulate appropriate responses to lifelike scenarios about acting as role models.

Materials:
Paper, pencil, printed scenarios; one device with Tellagami app for each group.

Steps:
- Divide students into small groups.
- Give each group a scenario that will help students understand the Condition of Heroes.
    - **Scenario 1:** Recently, a student told you that she does did not want to help you with your homework because you might take her answers. What do you do? What does it take to develop trust with your friends and teachers? Who do you trust? Why?
    - **Scenario 2:** During a group project, some students are not sharing their ideas or thoughts. You start to become frustrated because you think they are not helping. Why might these students not be participating? What can you do to help everyone feel comfortable with sharing his or her ideas in the group?
    - **Scenario 3:** In your class, students always interrupt each other. Students do not listen to each other's ideas or listen to each other's opinions. Why do you think students are disrespectful of other students at times? What can you do to model respectful behavior?
    - **Scenario 4:** There is a new student in your class. You already have your group of friends though. How could you be a Hero to the new student? What does it feel like to be a new student?

> **Common Core:**
> CCSS.ELA-LITERACY.CCRA.W.4 Produces clear and coherent writing in which the development, organization, and style are appropriate to task, purpose, and audience.
>
> **21st Century Skills:**
> Critical Thinking and Problem Solving, Leadership and Responsibility, Social and Cross-Cultural Interaction
>
> **ISTE/NETS:**
> Critical thinking, problem solving, and decision making D
> Digital citizenship B
> Technology operations and concepts A
> Creativity and innovation A, B, C

Source: Created using Tellagami.

- **Scenario 5:** You notice that a lot of the other students talk with the adults at your school. You don't really have an adult at school you could go to when you have a problem. How can you get to know more adults in your school? Who is one adult that you would like to get to know better?
- **Scenario 6:** Your teacher talks with other students and listens to them. However, you feel like your teacher does not pay attention to you. What could you do to help your teacher get to know you better? How could you participate more in class?

- Have students individually write out their answers and ideas for the scenario their group has been assigned. Then, have them share their individual answers with their group. Students should combine ideas to form an answer that captures the group's thinking.
- Next, have students create a cartoon using the Tellagami app. Students will pick a character, the character's clothing, background, and emotion. Then students can write text and record their voice.
- Next, each group will present their Tellagamis.

Personal Reflection:

In the form of an exit slip, students should describe a scenario like the ones in the activity from an actual experience they have had. They should provide any relevant background information. They should also explain how they handled the situation and whether their actions were Herolike.

Group Reflection:

As each group presents their Tellagami, ask the other groups if they would handle the scenario similarly. Would any handle the situation differently? Have other groups give their opinions.

Discuss the following questions:

- Have any of these scenarios happened to you before? How did you handle them?
- What do you do to show your friends and teachers you care about them?
- How are you a Hero?
- Who do you know that is a Hero?
- What does it mean to respect other students?
- When do you feel respected at school?

Extended Learning:

Have each group write an original scenario. Collect each scenario. Next, redistribute the student-created scenarios, making sure each group does not get their own scenario. Have each student write a response.

Please cut out scenario strips and give to each group.

Scenario 1: Recently, a student told you that she does did not want to help you with your homework because you might take her answers. What do you do? What does it take to develop trust with your friends and teachers? Who do you trust? Why?

My idea:

Group brainstorm:

Scenario 2: During a group project, some students are not sharing their ideas or thoughts. You start to become frustrated because you think they are not helping. Why might these students not be participating? What can you do to help everyone feel comfortable with sharing his or her ideas in the group?

My idea:

Group brainstorm:

Scenario 3: In your class, students always interrupt each other. Students do not listen to each other's ideas or listen to each other's opinions. Why do you think students are disrespectful of other students at times? What can you do to model respectful behavior?

My idea:

Group brainstorm:

Scenario 4: There is a new student in your class. You already have your group of friends though. How could you be a Hero to the new student? What does it feel like to be a new student?

My idea:

Group brainstorm:

Scenario 5: You notice that a lot of the other students talk with the adults at your school. You don't really have an adult at school you could go to when you have a problem. How can you get to know more adults in your school? Who is one adult that you would like to get to know better?

My idea:

Group brainstorm:

Scenario 6: Your teacher talks with other students and listens to them. However, you feel like your teacher does not pay attention to you. What could you do to help your teacher get to know you better? How could you participate more in class?

My idea:

Group brainstorm:

Copyright © 2015 by Corwin. All rights reserved. Reprinted from *Student Voice: Turn Up the Volume K–8 Activity Book* by Russell J. Quaglia, Michael J. Corso, and Julie Hellerstein. Thousand Oaks, CA: Corwin, www.corwin.com. Reproduction authorized only for the local school site or nonprofit organization that has purchased this book.

Grades K-2: Heroes Activities

My Everyday Super Hero Cartoon

(30–40 MINUTES)

Heroes:

Having people who believe in you and are there for you when you need them. Heroes are people who care about each other and support each other just as friends do every day. This activity encourages students to create an everyday Hero.

Objective:

Students will be able to identify and illustrate a characteristic that an everyday Hero possesses. Students will be able to draw an exaggerated feature to emphasize an important point.

Materials:

Large sheets of paper, markers; or iPads with ShowMe app.

> **Common Core:**
> CCSS.ELA-LITERACY.RL.1.1 Ask and answer questions about key details in a text.
> CCSS.ELA-LITERACY.RL.1.2 Retell stories, including key details, and demonstrate understanding of their central message or lesson.
>
> **21st Century Skills:**
> Creativity and Innovation, Communication
>
> **ISTE/NETS:**
> Communication and collaboration A
> Creativity and innovation B

Steps:

- Read the book *Do Super Heroes Have Teddy Bears?* by Carmela Coyle.
- Discuss the book: Why do the everyday Heroes or good citizens matter the most?
- Explain that everyday Heroes can be friends, parents, teachers, grandparents, neighbors, students, anyone. Brainstorm characteristics that everyday Heroes have such as helping others and listening.
- Have each student pick one trait from the list.
- Have students draw a picture of a Superhero that has this trait. Students should choose to focus or exaggerate the trait they picked.
- Show the class an example of everyday Superhero cartoon. For example, a Hero that loves to help might have really big helping hands.
- Next students will draw their everyday Superhero. If students have access to iPads or devices, use the ShowMe app to have students draw and record an explanation of their picture. Students may also create a drawing with markers and paper and give an oral presentation for their assessment.
- Have students share their everyday Superhero cartoons.

Source: Created using ShowMe.

Personal Reflection:

- How can you be a Hero to your friends?
- Who do you know that is a Hero?
- What do you have in common with these everyday Superheroes?

Group Reflection:

- What does it mean to respect people?
- When do you feel respected?
- What will you do to be a Hero to your friends, family, and teachers?

Extended Learning:

Students will decorate Superhero capes for their teddy bears or themselves with words and pictures that describe everyday Hero characteristics. Decorate a bandana or small piece of fabric.

Have students share the ShowMe drawings with classmates and family members.

Notes:
___
___
___
___
___
___
___
___

Grades K-2: Heroes Activities

Hall of Fame

(30–40 MINUTES)

Heroes:
Having people who believe in you and are there for you when you need them.

Objective:
Based on an interview or a biography, students will identify character traits in an individual and summarize a person's accomplishments.

Materials:
Graphic organizer, crayons, markers; frame materials—craft sticks, yarn.

Steps:
- Have students select a K–2 biography about a historic Hero from the library or media center. Alternatively, read several biographies out loud to students.
- As the biography is read, have students look for important events in this person's life.
- Hero Hall of Fame Graphic Organizer: Have students write the Hero's name, draw one important accomplishment in this person's life, and explain their drawing. They should also identify key traits of the Hero and write an explanation of why they admire this person. Next, students should draw a portrait of this person and create a frame around the portrait.
- Create a Hero Hall of Fame in your classroom. Students can hang up their Heroes' portraits in the Hall of Fame.
- Challenge students to add their favorite everyday Heroes to the Hall of Fame throughout the year.
- Students can create an Everyday Hero Hall of Fame following the graphic organizer above. They can interview their Hero about important accomplishment in his or her life and write down key traits and why they admire this person.
- Invite students to take turns inducting their Heroes into the Hall of Fame.

> **Common Core:**
> CCSS.ELA-LITERACY.RI.1.1 Ask and answer questions about key details in a text.
> CCSS.ELA-LITERACY.RI.1.2 Identify the main topic and retell key details of a text.
> CCSS.ELA-LITERACY.RI.1.3 Describe the connection between two individuals, events, ideas, or pieces of information in a text.
>
> **21st Century Skills:**
> Leadership and Responsibility, Communication
>
> **ISTE/NETS:**
> Research and information fluency A, B, C,
> Creativity and innovation B

Personal Reflection:

- What traits do you share with the Hero you inducted to the Hall of Fame?
- What did you learn from this person?

Group Reflection:

Why is it important to have a Hero?

Extended Learning:

Have a Heroes Hall of Fame induction celebration. Students will invite their everyday Hero for a celebration. Have students create a unique ribbon, badge, or certificate for their Hero as a token of their appreciation. Take a picture of each student and their Hero. At the induction ceremony, students should explain why they admire this person and what they learned from their Hero. There can also be a tour of the Heroes Hall of Fame led by students. Give the "Heroes" an opportunity to talk about who they admire and why.

Notes:

Hero Hall of Fame

Name _____

Name of Hero:

Drawing of Hero's accomplishment:

Explain the drawing:

Grades K-2: Heroes Activities

We Can Be Heroes—Me and You

(20–30 MINUTES)

Common Core:
CCSS.ELA-LITERACY.W.1.3
Write narratives in which they recount two or more appropriately sequenced events, include some details regarding what happened, use temporal words to signal event order, and provide some sense of closure.

21st Century Skills:
Critical Thinking and Problem Solving, Communication, Collaboration

ISTE/NETS:
Critical thinking, problem solving, and decision making D

Heroes:
Having people who believe in you and are there for you when you need them.

Objective:
Students will be able to develop strategies to deal with different social scenarios related to the Condition of Heroes.

Materials:
Scenario cards, materials for writing, drawing, or acting.

Steps:
- Explain to students that students can be Heroes.
- Invite students to imagine they are in different situations. Students can decide what they would do as a student Hero.

Use the following prompts for discussion, drawing, acting, or writing:

- Your teacher asks the class to be quiet but your friend keeps talking to you. What do you do?
- You are at recess with your two best friends, Katie and Brittany. Katie walks away, and Brittany starts telling a mean story about Katie. What do you do?
- A student at recess tripped and scraped his knee. What do you do?
- A student who can be mean and always acts like she is right makes a simple mistake while reading. The other students start to laugh. What do you do?
- You borrowed an eraser from the teacher and lost it. What do you do?
- The school janitor always cleans up and keeps the school nice. You see him in the hall. What do you do?
- You always forget to raise your hand and you talk out of turn. What should you do?
- A student is being made fun of on the playground. What do you do?

- A new student is sitting alone. What do you do?
- Someone in your class did not clean up the toys. What do you do?
- No one ever picks a student in your class to be partners. What do you do?
- You saw mean writing in the bathroom. What do you do?
- You're in line at lunch and you are really hungry. You see a friend of yours way ahead of you in line. Should you ask your friend if you can cut in line? What do you do?
- You find someone's toy on the playground. What do you do?
- You spill juice all over the classroom book. Your teacher isn't looking. Do you put it away? What do you do?
- A student in your class is learning English as his second language. He is usually really quiet. What do you do?

Personal Reflection:

- When have you been a Hero? What situation were you in?

Group Reflection:

Have students sit in a circle and share a story about when they acted like a Hero. Next, have students share about a time when they witnessed someone else be a Hero.

Extended Learning:

- Being a Hero is about showing respect. Watch the Pixar video *For the Birds* at https://www.youtube.com/watch?v=MOiyD26cJ2A. When were the birds disrespectful? What movies and books have taught you about respect? Find and share another video that helps you understand the concept of Heroes and respect better.
- Make the school a better place! As a class, be Heroes by making your school greener. Encourage students to recycle and pick up their trash. Plant a class garden or plant a tree to make the school a better place.
- Have your class get involved with a buddy program with students from another grade.

Notes:
_____
_____
_____
_____

Your teacher asks the class to be quiet but your friend keeps talking to you. What do you do?	You are at recess with your two best friends, Katie and Brittany. Katie walks away, and Brittany starts telling a mean story about Katie. What do you do?	A student at recess tripped and scraped his knee. What do you do?
A student who can be mean and always acts like she is right makes a simple mistake while reading. The other students start to laugh. What do you do?	You borrowed an eraser from the teacher and lost it. What do you do?	The school janitor always cleans up and keeps the school nice. You see him in the hall. What do you do?
You always forget to raise your hand and you talk out of turn. What should you do?	A student is being made fun of on the playground. What do you do?	A new student is sitting alone. What do you do?
Someone in your class did not clean up the toys. What do you do?	No one ever picks a student in your class to be partners. What do you do?	You saw mean writing in the bathroom. What do you do?
You're in line at lunch and you are really hungry. You see a friend of yours way ahead of you in line. Should you ask your friend if you can cut in line? What do you do?	You spill juice all over the classroom book. Your teacher isn't looking. Do you put it away? What do you do?	A student in your class is learning English as his second language. He is usually really quiet. What do you do?

Copyright © 2015 by Corwin. All rights reserved. Reprinted from *Student Voice: Turn Up the Volume K–8 Activity Book* by Russell J. Quaglia, Michael J. Corso, and Julie Hellerstein. Thousand Oaks, CA: Corwin, www.corwin.com. Reproduction authorized only for the local school site or nonprofit organization that has purchased this book.

CHAPTER 3

Sense of Accomplishment

> Every Friday is Finalize Friday. A modified schedule creates a forty-five-minute block of time for students to revisit work they have done during the past week to revise and improve any work they feel did not represent their best effort. Tests can be retaken, homework can be redone, and essays redrafted. This is not a time to catch up on missed or incomplete work. Rather, it is a time to demonstrate determination in bettering work already undertaken. Students not only improve their grades in this process but also learn the value of perseverance.

Consider how often you or your school recognizes and celebrates a student's achievement—that is to say, *what* they produce. Most schools do a good job of holding honor roll assemblies to reward academic achievement and awards banquets to reward athletic achievement. Some schools even have art fairs, where those who produce excellent works of art are recognized and noted with ribbons. This is important and should continue. In addition, schools should also be places that recognize and celebrate effort, perseverance, good citizenship, and all the many talents and gifts that students possess. A Sense of Accomplishment comes not just from having crossed the finish line first but from the effort put into running the race well.

First of all, effort and perseverance count for more toward the attainment of a person's aspirations than achievement. Getting all As may be easy for some students, whereas getting a solid C through hard work and study may be a challenge for others. Scoring touchdowns may be second nature to a young man who hit the genetic lottery, while just making the team requires hours of working out and preparation for another. It turns out that in life, this latter set of characteristics—those currently associated with *grit*—is more associated with success than the end product that typically gets so much attention in school.

Secondly, being a good citizen of the school is touted as important in mission statements and by administrators, yet how often are kindness and thoughtfulness applauded and upheld? It is easy to pay lip service to the behavioral ideals expressed in values statements and codes of conduct, but rarely are those who go out of their way to help and support others given the same recognition as those who excel academically or athletically.

Thirdly, while our students are multitalented, the set of talents celebrated in schools is fairly narrow. Frequently, those who are exceptional in the classroom or on the field have recognition assemblies, while those with as exceptional talent in music or theater or dance or comedy or photography or interpersonal relationships or preparing food or skateboarding or . . . —you get the idea—look on from the audience.

The following exercises will help you and your students see beyond what they achieve as a hallmark of success and look at the effort and perseverance that go into being successful. The exercises also help students expand the categories of what counts for accomplishment. Together you will learn that, although the primary purpose of school involves academics, academics need not be the only category in which we celebrate one another.

Grades 6-8: Sense of Accomplishment Activities

Marble Roll

(ABOUT 30 MINUTES)

Sense of Accomplishment:

Sense of Accomplishment is about celebrating the importance of effort and perseverance as signs of your success. The Condition is about trying repeatedly and facing challenges rather than giving up. Sense of Accomplishment is about all your talents and skill rather than just skills that are measured by tests and grades.

Objective:

Students will be able to discuss the importance of effort and perseverance. Students will be able to reflect on what is valued in school.

Materials:

Half a paper towel roll cut lengthwise for every student; four or five marbles; *Famous Failures* YouTube video, Edmodo (for extended learning).

> **Common Core:**
> CCSS.ELA-LITERACY.SL.6-8.1 Initiate and participate effectively in a range of collaborative discussions (one-on-one, in groups, and teacher-led) with diverse partners on grades 6-8 topics, texts, and issues, building on others' ideas and expressing their own clearly and persuasively.
>
> **21st Century Skills:**
> Communication, Collaboration
>
> **ISTE/NETS:**
> Communication and collaboration D

Steps:

- Divide students into teams of five to seven. Give each student a half tube and have teams stand at one end of the room.
- Establish a starting point (A) and an ending point (B). The distance can be about the length of a standard classroom.
- Tell students that the challenge is to move the marble from one end of the room to the other using the half paper tube. Have students line up and start the marble by rolling it down the half tube toward his or her teammate. The next person on the team catches the marble in his or her tube and proceeds to roll it and drop it into the next person's tube. Continue doing this until the team reaches point B. Students cannot carry the marble in their tube.
- Tell teams they will receive a grade for this activity. However, do not tell them what you are grading. Instead of a traditional grade that rewards the team who came in first with an A, second B, and so on, distribute grades based on teamwork, effort, perseverance, or having the most fun.

- Follow up with the video *Famous Failures* on YouTube. Ask: What did these famous people do after they experienced failure? Lead a discussion about the importance of effort and perseverance. How do these characteristics affect schoolwork? What does effort or perseverance look like in school?

Personal Reflection:

Reflect on a time that you wanted to give up because an assignment or task was too hard.

- What strategies did you use to overcome this frustration?
- Why did you put forth effort on this project? What was the outcome?

Group Reflection:

- Were you surprised by your groups' grade in the marble activity? Why or why not?
- What accomplishments are typically recognized in schools? In addition to those accomplishments, what other types of accomplishments should be recognized?
- Why are effort and hard work important?

Extended Learning:

Based on the *Famous Failures* video, students can identify and research a person who has illustrated great perseverance and effort. Students should write a brief report on what motivated the person, how the person persevered or showed effort, and what the outcome was. Students can share their report on Edmodo or a social media network of their choice. Students can also evaluate the perseverance of a historical character and discuss on Edmodo.

Notes:
_____
_____
_____
_____
_____
_____
_____

Grades 6-8: Sense of Accomplishment Activities

Student Actions

(INITIAL ACTIVITY: 20–30 MINUTES; FOLLOW-UP A FEW DAYS LATER: 20–30 MINUTES)

Sense of Accomplishment:

Sense of Accomplishment is about celebrating the importance of effort and perseverance as signs of your success. The Condition is about trying repeatedly and facing challenges rather than giving up. Sense of Accomplishment is about all your talents and skill rather than just skills that are measured by tests and grades.

Objective:

Students will be able to execute an action step or plan to improve their Sense of Accomplishment.

Materials:

List of student actions related to Sense of Accomplishment to post online, on board, or handouts for students.

Steps:

- Start with a discussion about Sense of Accomplishment: What does it feel like to persevere? How do you see students putting forth effort at school? Why do you think it is important for students to be good citizens? What could you do today to be a better citizen at school or in your community? What can you do to develop the Condition of Sense of Accomplishment for yourself?
- Tell students that they will take action to develop the Condition of Sense of Accomplishment. Post and review the following list of student actions on the board or create a shared Google document:
  - Revise an assignment just to improve your own understanding.
  - Tutor a peer or friend who is struggling in a certain subject.
  - If you are not an avid reader, read a book of your choice just for yourself.
  - Make a to-do list every day for one week. To what extent did you reach your goals?

Common Core:
CCSS.ELA-LITERACY.SL.6-8.1 Initiate and participate effectively in a range of collaborative discussions (one-on-one, in groups, and teacher-led) with diverse partners on grades 6-8 topics, texts, and issues, building on others' ideas and expressing their own clearly and persuasively.

CCSS.ELA-LITERACY.W.9-8.4 Produce clear and coherent writing in which the development, organization, and style are appropriate to task, purpose, and audience.

21st Century Skills:
Collaboration, Initiative and Self-Direction, Leadership and Responsibility

ISTE/NETS:
Communication and collaboration B, D

- Set a physical goal for yourself like running a 5k race. Log your training and preparation. Reflect on the experience. How did you feel a Sense of Accomplishment?
- Organize your school folders, notebooks, binders, or device.
- Solve a difficult Sudoku puzzle.
- When a task seems overwhelming, don't give up.
- Ask a teacher for suggestions and feedback beyond a letter grade.
- Get a new high score on a game.
- Solve a difficult math problem.
- Create a social media post of something you are proud of!
- Watch a movie or TV show where the character experiences a Sense of Accomplishment because of his or her perseverance, hard work, or citizenship.
- Create a Sense of Accomplishment poster or bulletin board with quotes, pictures, or a list of related traits. Be sure to get permission from teacher or school staff.
- Write a goal and put it in your shoe. When you accomplish it, rip it up and write a new one.
- Create a loom bracelet, figure out how to knit, or learn another hands-on craft.
- Finish something that you started a while ago but never got to.
- Hang up your schoolwork on your refrigerator, in your locker, or in your room. Make sure it is work where you improved or gave good effort!
- Write in your planner one thing that you are proud of every day for one month.

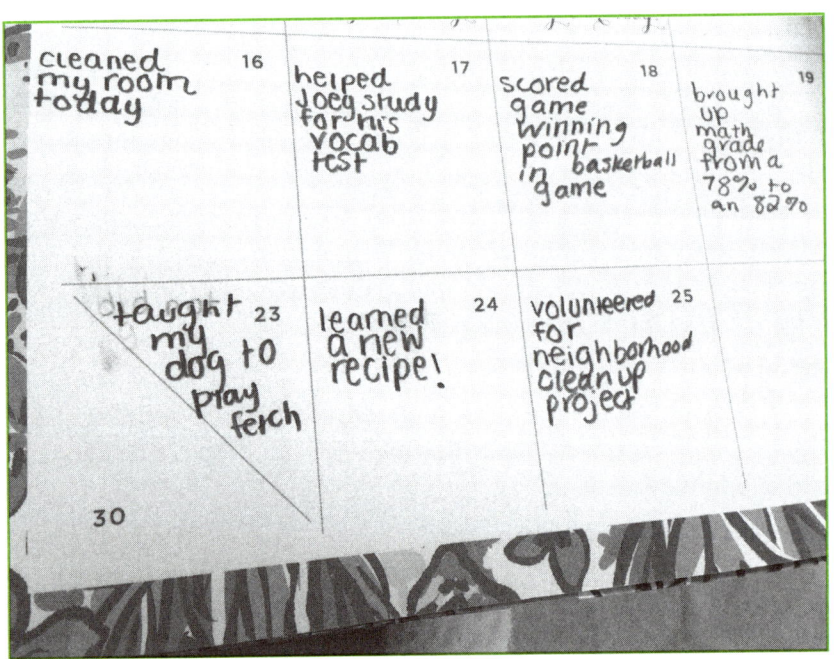

Source: Photo by Julie Hellerstein.

- Create a list of what you accomplished this year, this month, this week, and today.
- Work ahead on a long-term project for school.
- Clean your room. Take a before and after picture and compare.
- Participate in a community service activity.

* As you review the list, invite students to create other ideas on how they can have a Sense of Accomplishment.
* Have students sign up for the Sense of Accomplishment task of their choice. You may decide more than one student can do a task.
* Create a class list to hold students accountable to their action.
* Students should document or record their evidence of their action through video recording, audio recording, pictures, or journal reflection.
* Debrief the purpose of the activity and establish a due date.

Personal Reflection:

How did your action help foster the Condition of Sense of Accomplishment?

Group Reflection:

Students should share what they learned from undertaking the above actions in a large group. Then, break students into small groups. Have students read and discuss the statements below to guide a discussion or debate. Students should pay attention whether their peers have different ideas about each statement.

* Effort is just as important as getting good grades.
* Adults only care about good grades.
* Tests are not the only way to see if I know something.
* Good grades are most important factor for college.
* It is important to be involved with community service.
* Trying harder doesn't mean I will do better.
* Some students get good grades even though they put forth little effort.

Extended Learning:

Create a whole-school challenge for every student to take an action step that fosters the condition of Sense of Accomplishment. Find an effective way to communicate challenges with the rest of the student body.

* Create a Twitter account that posts different Sense of Accomplishment challenges.
* Ask the school website to post the list or pass out action cards at lunch.
* Create a bulletin board inviting students to try actions.

Revise an assignment just to improve your own understanding.	Tutor a peer or friend who is struggling in a certain subject.	Clean your room or organize your locker. Take a before and after picture and compare.	Make a to-do list every day for one week. To what extent did you reach your goals?
Set a physical goal for yourself like running a 5k race. Log your training and preparation. Reflect on the experience. How did you feel a Sense of Accomplishment?	Organize your school folders, notebooks, binders, or device.	Solve a difficult Sudoku puzzle.	When a task seems overwhelming, don't give up.
Ask a teacher for suggestions and feedback beyond a letter grade.	Get a new high score on a game.	Solve a difficult math problem.	Create a social media post of something you are proud of!
Watch a movie or TV show where the character experiences a Sense of Accomplishment because of his or her perseverance, hard work, or citizenship.	Create a Sense of Accomplishment poster or bulletin board with quotes, pictures, or a list of related traits. Be sure to get permission from teacher or school staff.	Write a goal and put it in your shoe. When you accomplish it, rip it up and write a new one.	Create a loom bracelet, figure out how to knit, or learn another hands-on craft.
Finish something that you started a while ago but never got to.	Hang up your schoolwork on your refrigerator, in your locker, or in your room. Make sure it is work where you improved or gave good effort!	Write in your planner one thing that you are proud of every day for one month.	Create a list of what you accomplished this year, this month, this week, and today.

Copyright © 2015 by Corwin. All rights reserved. Reprinted from *Student Voice: Turn Up the Volume K–8 Activity Book* by Russell J. Quaglia, Michael J. Corso, and Julie Hellerstein. Thousand Oaks, CA: Corwin, www.corwin.com. Reproduction authorized only for the local school site or nonprofit organization that has purchased this book.

Grades 6-8: Sense of Accomplishment Activities

Headline News

(ABOUT 50 MINUTES)

Sense of Accomplishment:

Sense of Accomplishment is about recognizing all the things students do that are accomplishments. Students should be proud of their accomplishments whether they are big or small. This activity encourages students to realize that accomplishments can be more than good grades and sports trophies.

Objective:

Students will be able to plan, write, and format a digital newspaper article about their accomplishments in a clear and coherent manner.

Materials:

Computers or devices with newspaper template of your choice. Free template available at http://www.readwritethink.org/files/resources/interactives/Printing_Press/.

Free templates are also available on Google docs.

Steps:

In this activity, students will write a front page for their own newspaper that highlights their accomplishments. Students have all kinds of accomplishments like being a good citizen, working hard, persevering, not giving up on a difficult task.

- Warm-up activity: Students will answer the following questions: What have you accomplished this school year? this month? this week? What accomplishments have you been recognized for in school or in the community? What is something you want to accomplish this year?

- Explain to students that they will be creating a newspaper that highlights their accomplishments. Bring in newspapers for students to view. Students can also review newspaper articles online. Students will select a front-page story and describe what makes it interesting.

> **Common Core:**
> CCSS.ELA-LITERACY.W.6.2
> Write informative/explanatory texts to examine a topic and convey ideas, concepts, and information through the selection, organization, and analysis of relevant content.
>
> CCSS.ELA-LITERACY.W.6.2.A
> Introduce a topic; organize ideas, concepts, and information, using strategies such as definition, classification, comparison/contrast, and cause/effect; include formatting (e.g., headings), graphics (e.g., charts, tables), and multimedia when useful to aiding comprehension.
>
> CCSS.ELA-LITERACY.W.6.2.B
> Develop the topic with relevant facts, definitions, concrete details, quotations, or other information and examples.
>
> CCSS.ELA-LITERACY.W.6.2.C
> Use appropriate transitions to clarify the relationships among ideas and concepts.
>
> CCSS.ELA-LITERACY.W.6.2.D
> Use precise language and domain-specific vocabulary to inform about or explain the topic.
>
> CCSS.ELA-LITERACY.W.6.4
> Produce clear and coherent writing in which the development, organization, and style are appropriate to task, purpose, and audience.

CCSS.ELA-LITERACY.W.6.5
With some guidance and support from peers and adults, develop and strengthen writing as needed by planning, revising, editing, rewriting, or trying a new approach.

CCSS.ELA-LITERACY.W.6.6
Use technology, including the Internet, to produce and publish writing as well as to interact and collaborate with others; demonstrate sufficient command of keyboarding skills to type a minimum of three pages in a single sitting.

21st Century Skills:
Media Literacy, Critical Thinking Skills, Communication, Creativity and Innovation

ISTE/NETS:
Creativity and innovation B
Communication and collaboration B

- Discuss as a class: What makes a front-page story interesting? What strategies do effective journalists use?
- Students will develop a newspaper name, one headline article, and several shorter articles that illustrate their accomplishments. Students should include details, facts, and what kind of effort, traits, and skills were required.
- Students may use their warm-up activity as a starting point. Allow students time to think, plan, and create their front pages.
- Students will use a Word document newspaper template or other newspaper template to create a newspaper rough draft.
- With a partner, students should peer edit and give feedback.
- Encourage students to upload pictures that illustrate their stories.
- Hot off the presses! Post students' articles in your classroom or post on class website. If students' headline articles are in pdf, upload into youblisher.com to turn into a publication with flipping pages.

Personal Reflection:

- Why is it important to feel recognized for a variety of achievements?
- What is the best way for my peers, teachers, friends, and family to recognize me for these accomplishments?

Group Reflection:

Celebrating each other's headlines is a great way to acknowledge the accomplishments of our peers. How can we continue to celebrate all of our accomplishments?

Extended Learning:

Brainstorm, create, and implement a class procedure or system that routinely celebrates students for a variety of accomplishments.

Here are some ideas to get you started:

- Watch the video clip from *Legally Blonde 2, Snap Cup Builds Group Cohesion*. Design your own snap cup. Students will recognize peers accomplishments by writing down their achievements. Once a week, read the slips of paper aloud and have everyone snap along as a way to applaud each other.

- Create a class Twitter account that mentions students for their hard work and being good citizens. Students can Tweet about their peers and give them shout outs.
- Create a Hall of Fame board where students can post their accomplishments, hang artwork, and share assignments they are proud of.
- Award students tickets for participation. Tickets can be redeemed for a homework pass or other incentive.
- Create a Class Dojo system. Show the students the video on class dojo at http://teach2.classdojo.com/#!/launchpad. Visit this tool that tracks students' accomplishments like participation, helping others, persistence, teamwork, and staying on task. You can grant students dojo points. At the end of the day, students will find out how they have done and what they can improve. Students all get to create their own avatar too.

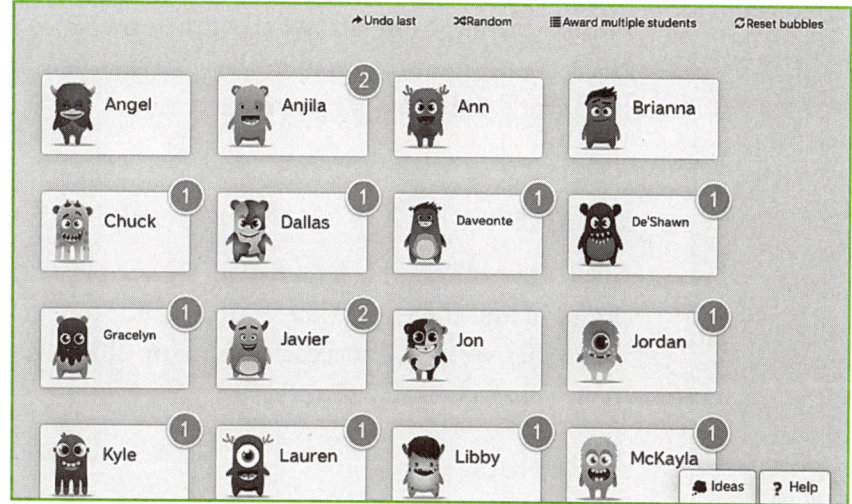

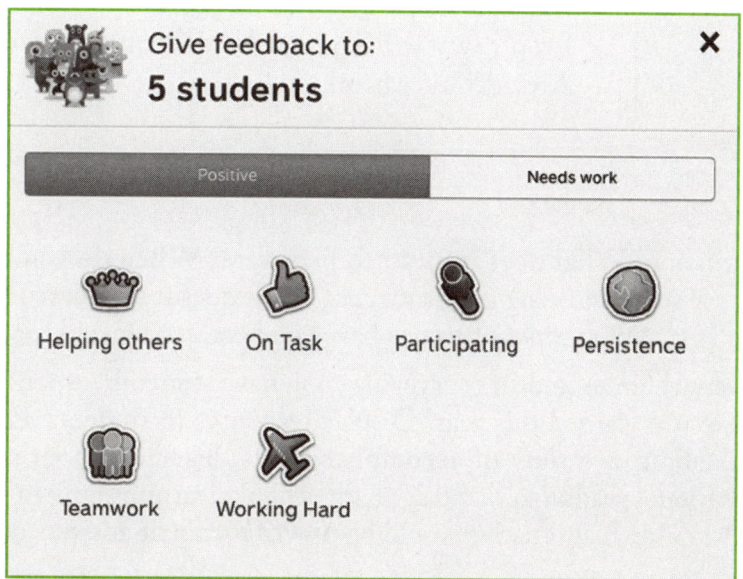

Source: Created using Class Dojo.

CHAPTER 3: SENSE OF ACCOMPLISHMENT

Grades 3-5: Sense of Accomplishment Activities

Award Show

(30–40 MINUTES)

Common Core:
CCSS.ELA-LITERACY.W.4.4
Produce clear and coherent writing in which the development and organization are appropriate to task, audience, purpose.

CCSS.ELA-LITERACY.SL.4.4
Report on a topic or text, tell a story, or recount an experience in an organized manner, using appropriate facts and relevant, descriptive details to support main ideas or themes; speak clearly at an understandable pace.

21st Century Skills:
Communication, Leadership and Responsibility, Social and Cross-Cultural Interaction

ISTE/NETS:
Digital citizenship B, D

Sense of Accomplishment:

Sense of Accomplishment is about recognizing all the things students do that are accomplishments. Students should be proud of their accomplishments whether they are big or small. It's about being recognized for many different types of success, including hard work and being a good citizen.

Objective:

Students will be able to explain an accomplishment they are proud of and the effort that went into it. Students will be able to argue that we are all successful in many different ways.

Materials:

Poll Everywhere or another survey tool; red paper or material for a red carpet; online award certificate maker like http://www.billybear4kids.com/show/awards/Online/AwardMaker.html.

Steps:

- Warm-up discussion: What does it mean to persevere? When do you try your best? When do you see students being good citizens? What does it feel like to be recognized for doing your best? What types of things have you been recognized for achieving?

- Using Poll Everywhere or another surveying tool, have students respond to the question: What have you learned this year? Display responses to students. Encourage students to think about a variety of accomplishments: learning about social studies, making a new friend, reading a difficult chapter book, learning how to be organized, for example. A low-tech alternative would be to write student answers on the board.

- Ask each student to think about something they are most proud of achieving and why they are most proud of achieving that. What hard work went into the accomplishment? What was the outcome? Students can write down their answers on a note card.

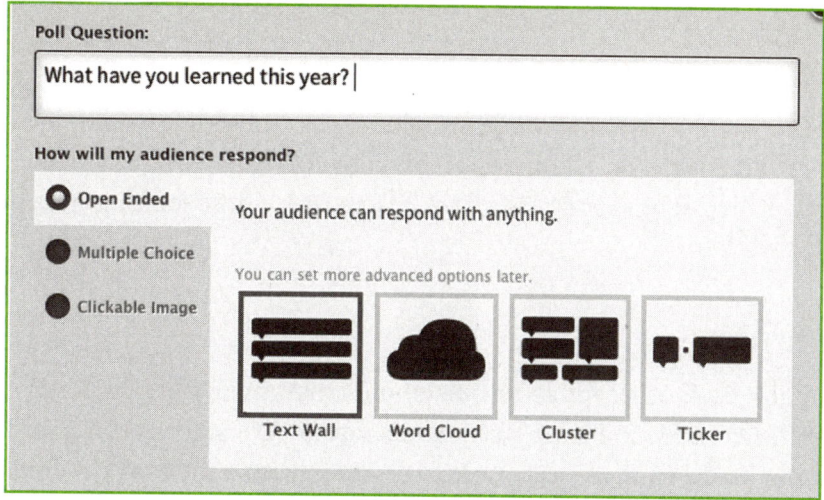

Source: Created using Poll Everywhere.

- Next, pair students and instruct students to create an online award certificate. Students will pick a border design, graphic, and describe the accomplishment by filling in a textbox. Then, have students practice presenting the information to their partner. Students will present these reasons in front of the class.
- Lay out the red carpet! Use red construction paper (long) or get red material and have students walk across the red carpet. Make sure the paparazzi captures candid photographs of your star students.
- Hold an awards ceremony. Have each student come up and present the award certificate to the student who was his or her partner. The student should briefly explain to the class what the awardee is proud of and what skills and effort went into the accomplishment. As recipients come up to accept their awards, they can thank their Heroes who helped them achieve their accomplishment. Make it like an award show by giving each student one minute. When one minute is up, play dramatic music to cue the student to finish. Have the audience clap and celebrate each student!

Personal Reflection:

- What did it feel like to be recognized for something you are proud of?
- Are all students successful in the same way or different ways? Explain and use examples.
- How can you recognize and support others for their accomplishments?

Group Reflection:

Students that feel a Sense of Accomplishment say

"I do not give up when I get frustrated."

"I complete homework and assignments."

"I help make the school a better place."

"I try my best at school."

Come up with other statements that students who feel a Sense of Accomplishment might say. Students can share these ideas on Edmodo, a class blog, or a shared Google document. Students can take a picture of themselves, and using PicCollage or a photo-editing app, write their statements in a thought bubble.

Extended Learning:

Continue to recognize each other for accomplishments that involve effort, perseverance, and good citizenship. Create a star jar! Get a large jar and decorate it with star stickers, paint, or other materials. Students can write down their peers' accomplishments on a piece of paper and place it in the star jar. Once a week, the teacher or a student could read the accomplishments aloud and celebrate these students!

Come up with your own personalized accomplishment system. Brainstorm with your class a way to recognize students' accomplishments. Use an online badge system to track accomplishments.

Notes:

Grades 3-5: Sense of Accomplishment Activities

How to . . .

(ABOUT 50 MINUTES, PRESENTATIONS ON FOLLOWING DAY)

Sense of Accomplishment:

Sense of Accomplishment is about recognizing all the things students do that are accomplishments. Students should be proud of their accomplishments whether they are big or small. It's about being recognized for many different types of success, including hard work and being a good citizen.

Objective:

Students will be able to design and teach a how-to lesson to the class.

Materials:

YouTube video: *How to Do the Cupid Shuffle Kids Hip Hop Moves.*

Steps:

- Share that we all are successful in different ways. Explaining and teaching someone else how to do something that you are proud of gives you a sense of accomplishment.

- Explain that we can all learn from each other. When you teach someone else to do something, it really shows that you are the expert and know it. Today, it is really easy for experts to share how to do something. Ask students if they have ever seen a how-to video before. Have students list examples.

- Next, show this sample of a how-to video, *How to Do the Cupid Shuffle Kids Hip Hop Moves* on YouTube. Play the video and have students learn the dance so they experience the step-by-step process. You may use a different step-by-step dance video if you would like.

> **Common Core:**
> CCSS.ELA-LITERACY.SL.4.4
> Report on a topic or text, tell a story, or recount an experience in an organized manner, using appropriate facts and relevant, descriptive details to support main ideas or themes; speak clearly at an understandable pace.
>
> CCSS.ELA-LITERACY.W.4.2
> Write informative/explanatory texts to examine a topic and convey ideas and information clearly.
>
> CCSS.ELA-LITERACY.W.4.2.D
> Use precise language and domain-specific vocabulary to inform about or explain the topic.
>
> **21st Century Skills:**
> Communication, Initiative and Self-Direction, Information Literacy
>
> **ISTE/NETS:**
> Creativity and innovation A, B
>
> Communication and collaboration A, B
>
> Research and information fluency B
>
> Technology operations and concepts A

- Explain to students that they will be teaching a skill in a how-to format like in the video.
- Have students brainstorm things that they know how to do and that they are proud of. For example, knowing how to play piano, solving a long division problem, making chocolate chip cookies, making a loom bracelet, tying their shoe, how to do a dance move, counting in Spanish. Students should think of a skill that they receive compliments about or something that they have done that others have not.
- Ask students to write down directions on how to do the thing that they are proud of. Give students time to outline their script and key points. Here are some reminders:
    - Be sure to have a title.
    - Explain what supplies are needed.
    - Write your instructions step by step.
    - Include any tips or special advice.
    - Proofread the instructions.
    - Practice your presentation.
- Option 1: Students could type their how-to steps and publish on the class website or other forum. Students should include links of other helpful websites related to their topic.
- Option 2: Students will present and teach the class!

Personal Reflection:

- What effort did you put into this assignment?
- What was the most difficult part of this assignment? How did you persevere?
- What kind of effort do you put into your school assignments? How could you put in more effort to your schoolwork?

Group Reflection:

- What did you learn from your classmates?
- How can we continue to learn from each other?
- How can we recognize everyone for his or her hard work, effort, and talents?

Extended Learning:

Students will create an actual how-to video using props or multimedia images to enhance their presentation. Use iMovie or another video tool of your choice.

Students will take an individual challenge that helps them feel a Sense of Accomplishment:

- Challenge yourself to do an assignment or problem you find difficult.
- Help a friend study for a test.
- Congratulate a friend who worked hard on an assignment.
- Pick up trash in the cafeteria.

- Become involved in a community service project.
- Organize your school folders.
- Create an award for a friend.
- Learn a new hobby or skill.
- Write down a to-do list and your goals in your planner. As you complete the items, cross them off!
- Write down your goals for the week, month, and year.
- Clean your room!

Notes:

Grades 3-5: Sense of Accomplishment Activities

Perseverance Phrase

(30–40 MINUTES)

Common Core:
CCSS.ELA-LITERACY.W.4.3.D
Use concrete words and phrases and sensory details to convey experiences and events precisely.

CCSS.ELA-LITERACY.W.4.10
Write routinely over extended time frames (time for research, reflection, and revision) and shorter time frames (a single sitting or a day or two) for a range of discipline-specific tasks, purposes, and audiences.

CCSS.ELA-LITERACY.SL.4.1.C
Pose and respond to specific questions to clarify or follow up on information, and make comments that contribute to the discussion and link to the remarks of others.

21st Century Skills:
Creativity and Innovation, Collaboration

ISTE/NETS:
Creativity and innovation A, B
Collaboration D

Sense of Accomplishment:

Sense of Accomplishment is about recognizing and awarding students who persevere even if the end result might not be the top grade or even a success. This activity challenges students to persevere in a task that might be challenging and frustrating.

Objective:

Students will be able to create a meaningful phrase that inspires students to persevere.

Materials:

Writing materials; access to the Internet; PicCollage or photo-editing tool.

Steps:

- Discuss perseverance: What does it mean to persevere? Why is it important to persevere during difficult tasks?
- List some people who have shown perseverance in literature and history.
- Thomas Edison wrote, "I never failed once when I invented the light bulb. It just happened to be a 2,000 step process." What did he mean by this quote?
- In small groups, have students research other quotes, slogans, or song lyrics on perseverance. Some examples are
  - "Just keep swimming."—Dory from *Finding Nemo*
  - "I think I can, I think I can."—*The Little Engine That Could*
  - "When you get to the end of your rope, tie a knot and hang on."—Franklin D. Roosevelt
  - "Just Do It!"—Nike
- In small groups, have students write their own motivational quote or slogan about perseverance.

- Encourage students to create a visual representation of this quote with the text. This can be achieved in PicCollage or another photo-editing app.
- Invite students to share their quotes with the class. Students should explain how this slogan or quote would help them persevere when they face a difficult task.

Personal Reflection:

- When have you faced a difficult task?
- How did you persevere? What was your motivation?
- What was the outcome? How did you feel?

Group Reflection:

- When is learning frustrating?
- Is it okay to try your hardest and still not be successful?
- Why is learning important itself even if you don't get a grade?
- What are tools and tips to deal with frustration?
- How do you find motivation to continue with a difficult task?
- How can you learn from these quotes and slogans?

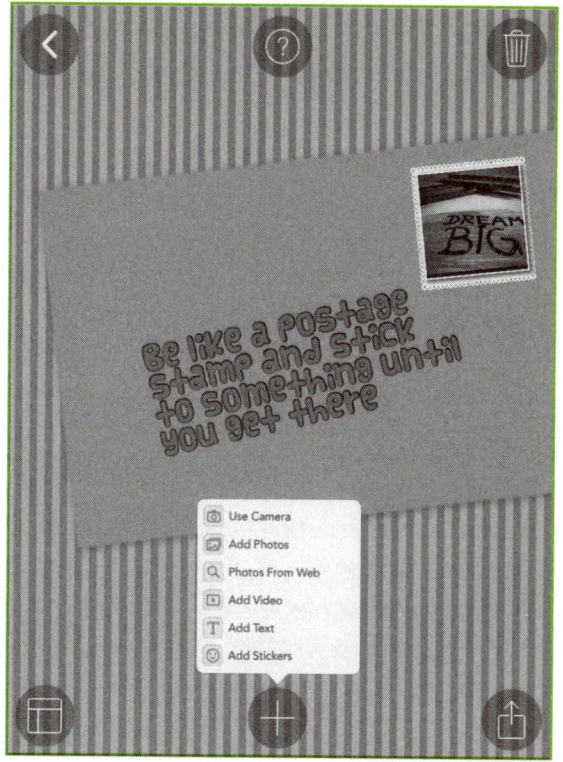

Source: Created using PicCollage.

Extended Learning:

Post this quote on the board: "Be like a postage stamp, stick to something until you get there!" —Josh Billings

Invite students to write down a goal that they will stick to until they get there.

Next, have students design their very own postage stamp that illustrates that goal.

You may decide to get white stickers to decorate, design a real postage stamp online, or have students draw their stamp on paper.

Learn more about stamps at http://www.postalmuseum.si.edu/educators/Design_It_Full_Curriculum.pdf.

Grades K-2: Sense of Accomplishment Activities

I Think I Can

(30–40 MINUTES)

Common Core:
CCSS.ELA-LITERACY.RLK-2.1 Ask and answer questions about key details in a text.

CCSS.ELA-LITERACY.RL.K-2.2 Retell stories, including key details, and demonstrate understanding of their central message or lesson.

CCSS.ELA-LITERACY.RL.K-2.3 Describe characters, settings, and major events in a story, using key details.

21st Century Skills:
Communication, Critical Thinking and Problem Solving, Initiative and Self-Direction

ISTE/NETS:
Creativity and innovation B
Digital citizenship B

Sense of Accomplishment:

Sense of Accomplishment recognizes perseverance and effort as signs of success.

Objective:

Students will be able to identify and evaluate a task that required perseverance.

Materials:

The Little Engine That Could book; train conductor hat paper template; tape, scissors.

Steps:

- Read *The Little Engine That Could* aloud to the class.
- Check for comprehension. Use think-pair-share to enhance student understanding. How do you think the little blue engine feels at the end of the story? Why? How do the children feel? How do the toys feel?
- Discuss the following questions: Why was it difficult for the little engine to go up the hill? Have you ever gone up a hill before? What do your legs feel like? This story teaches us how to overcome challenges. What are some difficult tasks in your life that you have completed? How did you get through it?
- Ask students to list things that are difficult for them.
- Have students write a goal that they think they can achieve by completing the sentence, "I think I can . . ." Provide examples like learning to write their name, read, add numbers, ride a bike, tie their shoes, learn to count in Spanish, and so on.
- Option: Purchase train conductor hats for students at a craft store or online.
- Next, have students draw a picture of them completing the goal using the Doodle Buddy app. Students can use the icons at the bottom of the app to take a picture, use a camera roll, or a preloaded background. Students can also add text. Use a variety of art

tools like chalk, glitter, and paint. Students can export their picture. Instruct students how to set the picture to their devices' background.

- Arrange the devices with the picture displayed in a line as if they were train cars. Allow students to view other students' goals.
- Invite students to line up holding each other's shoulders and move around the room saying "I think I can, I think I can."

Personal Reflection:

- When have you completed a hard task before?
- What did you tell yourself to get you through it?
- Is it important to believe in yourself?

Group Reflection:

- Is it important to have an "I think I can" attitude? Why?
- How can you give encouragement to yourself?
- How could you give encouragement to your friends?
- What advice would you give to a friend who says, "I can't" during a difficult task?
- Why is it important to give encouragement?

Extended Learning:

Discuss the following scenario: You notice that one of your classmates is struggling with reading. They can't seem to understand certain words or phrases. What encouragement could you give a friend who is having a difficult time at school? What encouragements have other people given to you to do your best? Create an encouragement digital card to give to a friend who is working on something difficult using punchbowl.com.

Notes:
_____
_____
_____
_____
_____

Grades K-2: Sense of Accomplishment Activities

Citizen Action Plan

(30–40 MINUTES)

Common Core:
CCSS.ELA-LITERACY.RLK-2.1 Ask and answer questions about key details in a text.

CCSS.ELA-LITERACY.RL.K-2.2 Retell stories, including key details, and demonstrate understanding of their central message or lesson.

CCSS.ELA-LITERACY.RL.K-2.3 Describe characters, settings, and major events in a story, using key details.

21st Century Skills:
Critical Thinking and Problem Solving

ISTE/NETS:
Critical thinking, problem solving, and decision making A, B, C, D

Sense of Accomplishment:

Sense of Accomplishment promotes the importance of being a good citizen. This activity encourages students to be good citizens all year and not just on special occasions.

Objective:

Students will be able to collaborate to form and follow a citizenship action plan.

Materials:

We Live Here Too by Nancy Loewen.

Steps:

- Warm-up discussion questions: What does it mean to be a good citizen? Why is it important to help the community? Does helping the community and others make you feel good or give you a sense of accomplishment?

- Read *We Live Here Too* by Nancy Loewen. In this book, students write letters to the neighborhood advice columnist who gives advice about how students can be good citizens in their schools and communities.

- Have students answer questions about the text, retell details, and describe the characters, settings, and key points.

- Next, ask students to write or ask their own questions about citizenship at school or in the community. Through this conversation, students should identify ways they could be better citizens at school.

- As a class, brainstorm ideas. For example, create a community garden, create a mural, collect school recycling bins, or pick up trash on the playground.

- Take action with one of the solutions. Form a long-term citizenship action plan where everyone can help.

Personal Reflection:

When have you helped someone else? How does it feel to help other people?

Group Reflection:

Discuss the following scenario: Your principal has announced that he or she wants all students to be good citizens. When you walk down the hallway, you notice that kids are dropping trash on the ground and not picking it up. What does it mean to be a good citizen in this case? How could you be a good citizen at school every day?

Extended Learning:

Document your citizenship plan and actions on video. Interview students on their actions and how it makes them feel. Share this with other classrooms and the community. Watch *Change the World in 5 Minutes—Everyday at School* at https://www.youtube.com/watch?v=oROsbaxWH0M for some inspiration!

Notes:

_____
_____
_____
_____
_____
_____
_____
_____
_____
_____
_____
_____

Grades K-2: Sense of Accomplishment Activities

Congratulations Card

(30–40 MINUTES)

Common Core:
CCSS.ELA-LITERACY.W.K.2
Use a combination of drawing, dictating, and writing to compose informative/explanatory texts in which they name what they are writing about and supply some information about the topic.

21st Century Skills:
Creativity and Innovation, ICT Literacy, Communication

ISTE/NETS:
Creativity and innovation B
Communication and collaboration B
Technology operations and concepts A, B, D

Sense of Accomplishment:
Sense of Accomplishment is about recognizing all the things we do that are accomplishments.

Objective:
Students will create a congratulations card for someone who has reached an achievement. Students will write and illustrate a greeting card.

Materials:
Cards, markers, encouraging word list.

Steps:

- Warm-up discussion: Why is it important to congratulate or say "Good job" to someone who has reached an achievement?
- When has someone said "Congrats!" or "Good job!" to you before?
- Explain that people sometimes send greeting cards to congratulate someone who has done a good job. Share a greeting card that you have received before. Explain how it made you feel, who sent it, and why. Ask students to share their experiences with greeting cards. Ask if they have ever sent or received a card. Ask: Why do people send cards?
- Identify a person in your life who has reached an achievement—big or small.

    a. a brother or sister received a good report card

    b. a cousin got a job

    c. a friend learned how to read

- Share examples of paper greeting cards. Allow students to research kid friendly e-greeting cards on the computer.
- Create a word and phrase list of positive affirmations—*Great job! Congratulations! Way to go! You are a hard worker!*

- Have students pay attention to language, writing style, rhyming, and illustrations.
- Invite students to design and create a greeting card for someone special who has accomplished something. The greeting card should have a clear message and purpose. The illustrations should match the text. Writing and punctuation should be appropriate. Students may create an electronic greeting card or a paper card.
- Use the Red Stamp app. Click "Say Happy." Then, click on Congratulations. Select a template and add pictures and text.
- Compare and contrast the difference between an electronic greeting card and a paper card.
- Assist students with sending their cards.

Personal Reflection:

- What types of things have you been recognized for achieving?
- Think of a range of your accomplishments. Pick the accomplishment you are most proud of.
- Create a congratulations card for yourself about your proudest accomplishment. Why did it make you proud? Why is it important to recognize your own achievements?

Source: Created using Red Stamp.

Group Reflection:

Have students present their greeting cards to the class. Discussion questions: Why is it important to celebrate all your accomplishments? Why is it important to recognize others' accomplishments? Reinforce that we can all be successful in many different ways.

Extended Learning:

Create a post office in your classroom. Students can continue to write and illustrate greeting cards throughout the year for their classmates and students and teachers in other classrooms about their accomplishments. Have students take turns being the mail person. Teach students how to deliver and sort mail.

Visit USPS Education Tools at http://about.usps.com/corporate-social-responsibility/connections.htm for education kits about stamps and postal service learning materials.

CHAPTER 4

Fun & Excitement

Very few people list sitting at a desk inside all day doing solo work on their top ten list of things to do for fun and excitement. While no doubt people work at office jobs they enjoy, most people find pleasure in being outside, moving around and being with other people. In addition to being engaged by such activities most people learn in such a setting. Whether it's learning about a friend's recent exploits while hiking together or learning a new handhold while rock climbing or learning about a new species of sea life at the beach, the outdoors and learning and fun go hand in hand in hand. At one pre-K-8 elementary school, they exploit the outdoor potential for learning every week. Each day two grades are outside for extended periods engaged in learning activities—pre-K and fourth grade on Mondays, Kindergarten and fifth grade on Tuesdays, and so on. Activities range from learning adjectives or writing poems about what they see, to counting chains on the swings or multiplying cars in the parking lot. Science plays a big part and so does art (chalk, spray painting, even mud sculptures). There is a school garden and a small greenhouse. Students learn and learn how much the outdoors has to teach.

We sometimes meet people in schools who believe seriousness and fun are mutually exclusive. That learning can only happen in an environment that is emotionally sterile. This runs counter to our experience and, by the way, a significant amount of research that makes a connection between emotional engagement and learning. While many teachers and students believe that learning can be fun, Fun & Excitement seems to get squeezed out of classrooms by rigid curriculum, strict pacing guides, and a do-or-die need to make adequate yearly progress (AYP). Fun, if it exists at all in schools, is relegated to extracurricular experiences like sports, clubs, and field trips.

Yet Fun & Excitement—affective engagement—is essential to sustain the focus and energy required to learn something deeply and well. Consider how difficult it is to learn material you find boring or to pay attention to someone who is dull no matter how important what they are saying is. The fact of the matter is our students are each a "whole child." That is to say, they come to us not just with an intellect, but also with emotions. Not just with thoughts, but with feelings. Not just with a mind, but also with a body that, during the school years, is growing and energetic and needs to move far more often than most children have a chance to when they are at school. We ourselves are better teachers when we reveal the passion we have for a particular subject or for learning itself. Students tell us all the time about how much they enjoy a class because of the obvious love of the subject matter the teacher has.

Creating a learning environment that is emotionally engaging is not about the teacher finding ways to entertain the students. Educators would have a hard time competing with the resources available to the entertainment industry. Nor, as with the other Conditions, is Fun & Excitement solely the teacher's responsibility. Students are responsible for behavior that can allow for fun without becoming chaotic, as well as for being in touch with their interests and passions as it connects to what is being studied. Together teachers and students can create classroom experiences that are both educational and enjoyable.

Fun & Excitement as a Condition that supports student aspirations is not about telling jokes or taking a break from studies to do something amusing that does not involve learning. Fun & Excitement is about ensuring the learning we are doing is engaging, that we are passionate about what we are studying, and that we connect to it on an emotional level. When Fun & Excitement is present in a classroom environment, time passes quickly as everyone becomes immersed in the learning experience. While not every lesson in every subject can be utterly engrossing every day, the following exercises will help you and your students discover the Fun & Excitement that is available to you while learning. Together you will explore how technology, social experiences, everyday relevance, and physical movement can reverse the boredom that might accompany otherwise traditionally dull experiences in school.

Grades 6-8: Fun & Excitement Activities

Heads Up!

(ABOUT 30 MINUTES)

Common Core:
CCSS.ELA-LITERACY.SL.7.1.C
Pose questions that elicit elaboration and respond to others' questions and comments with relevant observations and ideas that bring the discussion back on topic as needed.

21st Century Skills:
Collaboration, Communication, Creativity and Innovation, Critical Thinking and Problem Solving

ISTE/NETS:
Creativity and innovation A, B, D

Critical thinking, problem solving, and decision making A, B, C

Fun & Excitement:

Enjoying what you are doing whether at work, school, or play. Engaging students is the key to Fun & Excitement. Students learn better and enjoy learning more when they are actively involved in whatever they are learning.

Objective:

Students will be able to recall and describe class concepts to a classmate in an efficient and quick manner. Students will be able to suggest ways to make learning more engaging and fun.

Materials:

iPads or iPhones with Heads Up! app ($0.99); add the build your own deck feature ($0.99). You may decide to give each group an iTunes gift card and they will enter the code on their device, or ask for volunteers to buy the app (with parental permission). If you are using a school set of devices, check protocols with your IT department.

Steps:

- Explain to students that they are going to review for a test or quiz in an interactive, engaging way.
- Provide students a list of key concepts and vocabulary words or have students create a comprehensive list as a class.
- Students should get into groups of four. Each group should have one device with the Heads Up! app. Watch Ellen DeGeneres's video tutorial of the game. She explains that you pick a category or your own deck.
- **How the Game Works:** The person who is guessing first will hold up the device to his or her forehead. Other group members will give the student clues so he or she can guess the word. Students have sixty seconds to get as many words as possible.
- To begin playing, have students open the Heads Up! app. They should click Build Your Own Deck and create their deck by entering the words from the list generated earlier.

- Begin playing the game.
- The front camera and a mobile device records the whole session. After a round, have students watch the video of them explaining each word.
- Ask students to take turns and see who can get the most words correct in one minute.

Personal Reflection:

- Describe your engagement in this activity. Was it fun? How did you contribute to the fun? How could you make school more interesting?
- When do you find learning fun? When are you most engaged in learning?

Group Reflection:

Using a Google document or another collaborative list, have students share their ideas on how to improve learning in the classroom. Have a discussion on what makes learning fun and how to make something that is boring more exciting. Have students respond to each other's points and make relevant observations on the topic.

Extended Learning:

Invite students to work in teams to create a new learning review game using the appropriate classroom content. Encourage students to be creative. Students can incorporate physical activity, art, hands-on learning, competition, technology, and more to make it engaging. Next, have students teach other students how to play their game.

Notes:
_____
_____
_____
_____
_____
_____
_____
_____

Grades 6-8: Fun & Excitement Activities

Appy Hour

(40–50 MINUTES)

Common Core:
CCSS.ELA-LITERACY.SL.7.1 Engage effectively in a range of collaborative discussions.

CCSS.ELA-LITERACY.SL.8.4 Present claims and findings, emphasizing salient points in a focused, coherent manner with relevant evidence, sound valid reasoning, and well-chosen details; use appropriate eye contact, adequate volume, and clear pronunciation.

21st Century Skills:
Critical Thinking and Problem Solving, Communication, Collaboration, Media Literacy, Information Literacy

ISTE/NETS:
Creativity and innovation A, B

Communication and collaboration A, B, D

Critical thinking, problem solving, and decision making A, B, C, D

Digital citizenship B

Technology operations and concepts B

Fun & Excitement:

Enjoying what you are doing whether at work, school, or play. Engaging students is the key to Fun & Excitement. Students learn better and enjoy learning more when they are actively involved in whatever they are learning.

Objective:

Students will be able to present and teach on effective studying and learning applications and strategies.

Materials:

Devices with access to app store, Internet, Apple TV or projector for displaying.

Steps:

- Warm-up discussion about engagement and technology: Is technology a distraction to learning or a learning tool? How can technology increase your learning? When have you used technology in school? How have you learned with technology outside of the classroom?
- Ask students to research apps and technology that increase student learning, such as review games, educational programs, note taking apps, creation apps, interactive programs, or video games, for example.
- Students should pick one app or strategy to teach to the class. Students need to demonstrate how to use the app and explain how it makes learning more fun. Students should explain how the app helps them directly with classroom content.
- Next hold "Appy Hour." Invite students to present one app or technology strategy that helps them learn. Students should explain key features of the app and how it helps them be engaged and learn. Have each student present at the front of the class and connect their device to the projector. Have students celebrate after each presentation. You may decide to serve apple juice and apple snacks to make it like a restaurant happy hour.

- Allow time for question and answer.
- Encourage students to use these apps while studying or try to incorporate them into your classroom practices.

Personal Reflection:

Ask students to take a screen shot of their app and provide a summary of what the app does and how it connects to learning.

Source: © Goodluz/Thinkstock Photos

- Ask: What makes this app fun and interesting?
- Did this assignment change your perspective on the relationship between technology and learning?

Group Reflection:

Students can share their screen shots and summaries onto a classroom blog or forum like Edmodo. Students can post questions and comments about each app.

- What does it feel like to have fun at school?
- How do you see students enjoying learning?
- Why do you think school is boring at times?
- What can you do today to be more engaged in your learning at school?

Extended Learning:

Discuss the learning apps. What characteristics did they share? Did some require higher levels of thinking? Could you combine any features to make a super-learning app? As a class, come up with a new learning app that helps students understand what they are currently studying in class. Have them name the app, design the icon, and write a short description of what it does. Students who are interested in technology could proceed to make the app. There are many resources online to help.

Notes:
_____
_____
_____
_____

Grades 6-8: Fun & Excitement Activities

Un-Bored Games

(ABOUT 40 MINUTES)

Common Core:
CCSS.ELA-LITERACY.SL.6-8.1
Engage effectively in a range of collaborative discussions.

21st Century Skills:
Critical Thinking and Problem Solving, Creativity and Innovation, Communication, Collaboration

ISTE/NETS:
Creativity and innovation A, B

Communication and collaboration A, B, D

Critical thinking, problem solving, and decision making A, B, C, D

Fun & Excitement:

Enjoying what you are doing whether at work, school, or play. Engaging students is the key to Fun & Excitement. Perhaps nothing is more fun and exciting for students than to mix up rules and do things differently.

Objective:

Students will be able to modify existing rules to a board game. Students will be able to construct a new classroom rule that increases student engagement.

Materials:

One board game or card game for every four students, or online board games from http://www.pogo.com/board-games or another gaming site.

Steps:

- Have students bring in board or card games. These can be online or traditional games.
- Warm-up discussion: What subjects and assignments do you find fun and exciting at school? Explain.
- Post a list of school rules or your classroom rules. What rules do you think get in the way of school being a more exciting place for learning? Why do you think these rules prevent fun? Which rules support a fun learning environment?
- Divide students into random groups of three or four by using playing cards. You can match students based on suit or number depending on what works best with your number of students.
- Each group should pick a familiar board game and rewrite the rules of the game that they selected to make it even more fun.
- Instruct students to write out the new directions and new rules.
- Allow students to play their new game and share the new rules with the entire class.

Personal Reflection:

- Why do you think changing the rules of a game makes playing that game more fun?
- What rule changes would make professional sports more fun to watch?
- What new rules would promote Fun & Excitement in this class?

Group Reflection:

Students will think-pair-share with their responses from their personal reflection. Discuss what new rules would promote Fun & Excitement in this class. As a class, select one rule to implement that would increase student engagement for all students. Be sure to think through all of the implications for this rule. Add the rule to the syllabus. Have students brainstorm ways to enforce this rule.

Extended Learning:

What new rules would promote Fun & Excitement in school? Critically evaluate the student handbook rules for your school based on student learning and Fun & Excitement. Pick two rules. How do these rules promote or hinder Fun & Excitement for students? Write a rationale. Next, rewrite one rule to increase Fun & Excitement at school. If your new rule was in effect, how do you predict students would behave? How would this impact school faculty and students?

Research social contract theory. Use primary sources to guide discussion. Why are rules important for society? What rules promote social order? Who should benefit from rules or laws? What rules and laws in our government would you like to see changed? Explain an idea for a law that would increase Fun & Excitement in the workplace or schools.

Notes:

Grades 3-5: Fun & Excitement Activities

Build a Band

(20–30 MINUTES)

Common Core:
CCSS.ELA-LITERACY.SL 3-5.1
Engage effectively in a range of collaborative discussion

CCSS.ELA-LITERACY.SL.4.1.C
Pose and respond to specific questions to clarify or follow up on information, and make comments that contribute to the discussion and link to the remarks of others.

21st Century Skills:
Creativity and Innovation

ISTE/NETS:
Creativity and innovation B

Fun & Excitement:
Enjoying what you are doing whether at work, school, or play. Fun & Excitement is about having fun and enjoying school every day. This activity encourages students to have fun by creating a band with everyday objects.

Objective:
Students will compose music by using everyday objects and create lyrics related to a class concept.

Materials:
Variety of objects for each group: pencils, books, markers, jar full of paper clips, for example.

Steps:
- Warm-up discussion: How can music help you learn? How does music help people express themselves? What are some other ways people express themselves?
- Have students work in groups of four or five. Inform students that they will create a band. Ask students to name their band.
- The bands can use any available classroom objects as their instruments.
- Give bands time to find instruments and put together a short performance.
- Have students write lyrics that explain a concept that the class has recently learned. Students may choose to create their own beat or "cover" a familiar song.
- Concert time! Allow each band to perform for several minutes.

Personal Reflection:
- Does music help students learn? Explain.
- What else makes learning fun?
- Describe a project or assignment that was interesting to you. What made it interesting?

Group Reflection:

- How can music make learning more interesting?
- How else could we incorporate music into our classroom?

Extended Learning:

Have students create and record a song about classroom concepts or information using the GarageBand app. When finished, play the songs for the class to enjoy! Encourage dancing and physical movement to enhance the experience.

Students can create their own podcasts using GarageBand to explain classroom concepts or to read a story aloud. Have students add special effects and sound effects to make it more engaging.

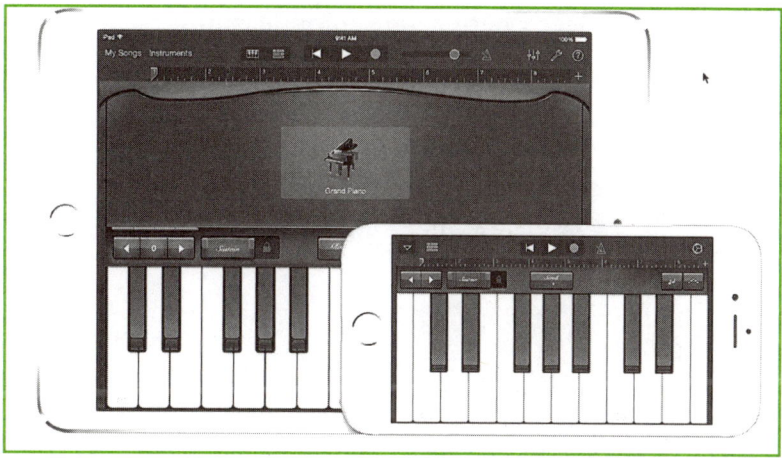

Source: Courtesy of GarageBand.

Check out Best Music Apps for Kids at https://www.commonsensemedia.org/lists/best-music-apps-for-kids.

Notes:

_____

_____

_____

_____

_____

Grades 3-5: Fun & Excitement Activities

Molding Minds

(30–40 MINUTES)

> **Common Core:**
> CCSS.ELA-LITERACY.SL.4.1.D Review the key ideas expressed and explain their own ideas and understanding in light of the discussion.
>
> **21st Century Skills:**
> Creativity and Innovation, Collaboration
>
> **ISTE/NETS:**
> Creativity and innovation B
> Communication and collaboration D
> Technology operations and concepts A, D

Fun & Excitement:

Enjoying what you are doing whether at work, school, or play. Engaging students is the key to Fun & Excitement. Students learn better and enjoy learning more when they are actively involved in whatever they are learning.

Objective:

Students will be able to express curricular concepts in an unconventional way.

Materials:

Play dough or clay; Hyperlapse app.

Steps:

- Discussion: What does a student look like who is fully involved in an activity? Have students strike a pose and act out what a student would look like who is engaged. Discuss. What does a student who is fully involved in an activity sound like? Have students call out some examples of what you might hear an engaged student say. Discuss. What does it feel like to be fully involved in an activity? What does it means to be excited about learning?
- Set up play dough building stations around the room. Assign three or four students to each station. Give each group one color of play dough.
- Students should create a team name based on the color play dough they have. Students should also come up with a team cheer. Next, give each group a topic, concept, or vocab word that the class has been studying.
- Give students fifteen minutes to plan and express their knowledge of the topic by using only play dough.
- While students work on their projects, use an iPhone or iPad to record the class. Use Hyperlapse app to record video. It will automatically speed up the movement. You will use this video to show your students what being fully involved in learning looks like.
- Invite students to share their work with the class.
- Next, project the video and discuss engagement.

Personal Reflection:

- Did you find you were fully interested in this kind of learning? Why or why not?
- What ideas do you have for making schoolwork more interesting for you?

Group Reflection:

- What makes building and creating fun?
- Brainstorm other opportunities for Fun & Excitement that increase student learning.
- What does Fun & Excitement while learning look like? Sound like? Feel like?

Extended Learning:

Students can create their own Hyperlapse videos to illustrate a concept and show progression, growth, or excitement. Students can adjust the speed. Encourage students to research examples: repairing a phone, students out in the hallway, kids playing at recess, crowds of people, cookies baking in an oven, cleaning your room, an airplane taking off, clouds, a plant growing.

Notes:
___
___
___
___
___
___
___
___
___
___

Grades 3-5: Fun & Excitement Activities

Story Starters

(30–40 MINUTES)

Common Core:
CCSS.ELA-LITERACY.SL.4.1.C
Pose and respond to specific questions to clarify or follow up on information, and make comments that contribute to the discussion and link to the remarks of others.

21st Century Skills:
Critical Thinking and Problem Solving, Collaboration, Flexibility and Adaptability

ISTE/NETS:
Creativity and innovation A, B
Communication and collaboration D

Fun & Excitement:

Enjoying what you are doing whether at work, school, or play. Thinking differently can be very fun and engaging.

Objective:

Students will be able to create a progressive story by collaborating and building on each other's ideas.

Materials:

Scene starter slips from books or personalized story starters based on your curriculum.

Steps:

- Tell students that they are going to play an improvisation game. Everyone will have a turn to tell the story and to act out his or her part.
- Break the class into two groups.
- Give each group a scene starter.
    - Story Starter 1: The school dance was completely ruined when . . .
    - Story Starter 2: I couldn't believe it when my teacher said we were going on a field trip to . . .
    - Story Starter 3: It was just like every other day during show and tell until Kevin brought in . . .
    - Story Starter 4: It was the most unusual recess we have ever had and it all began because we started to play . . .
    - Story Starter 5: Kyle and Brianna stood there in awe when they looked up and saw . . .
- Someone should start a scene based on the piece of paper you give him or her. Once the scene begins, the next person should continue the story but add a new direction to it. For example, if the scene starter is: "It was the last five minutes of the championship

baseball game . . ." the next person might add "Who knew, at that very moment that Brian was asking Riley to prom." A third student might continue by saying "As Casey stood their alone watching, she got an urgent phone call with the exciting news."

- Explain that the game involves continuing the story but taking it in a new direction.
- The story can also be told through writing. Create an Edmodo group for each story scene and have students add on to the story by adding comments.

Personal Reflection:

- Was it a challenge to think differently for this activity?
- Describe a real-life scenario where thinking differently could help you.

Group Reflection:

- What skills did you have to use for this activity? Why are these skills important?
- In the activity, was there a right or wrong answer?
- Was it difficult to think differently for this activity?
- What was it like thinking of a story on the spot?
- Together, create more scene starters.

Extended Learning:

Have students think differently through creative writing prompts. Invite students to visit http://www.scholastic.com/teachers/story-starters/. Have them select a story starter theme and type in their name and grade level. Tell them to spin the lever to get a fun, creative prompt such as "Write an e-mail to a dreadful mermaid who is looking for an invisible door." Have them pick the format. When they are finished they can e-mail or print their story!

Students can create their own storyboard on www.storyboardthat.com/storyboard-creator.

Notes:
_____
_____
_____
_____
_____

- Story Starter 1: The school dance was completely ruined when . . .

- Story Starter 2: I couldn't believe it when my teacher said we were going on a field trip to . . .

- Story Starter 3: It was just like every other day during show and tell until Kevin brought in . . .

- Story Starter 4: It was the most unusual recess we have ever had and it all began because we started to play . . .

- Story Starter 5: Kyle and Brianna stood there in awe when they looked up and saw . . .

1. Create your own:

2. Create your own:

Grades K-2: Fun & Excitement Activities

Scenarios

(30–40 MINUTES)

Fun & Excitement:
Enjoying what you are doing whether at work, school, or play.

Objective:
Students will be able to role-play scenarios related to Fun & Excitement at school.

Materials:
Graphic organizer sheet.

Steps:
- Distribute graphic organizer.
- Read through each scenario together. Have each student write or draw his or her answers to one scenario before reading the next. Allow students a few minutes for each scenario.
    - Scenario 1: Some of your friends always complain that school is boring. You enjoy school and have fun learning new things. How can you help your friends enjoy school more? What makes school fun for you?
    - Scenario 2: Your teacher assigns a project where you can learn and explore anything that interests you. What would you pick?
    - Scenario 3: Some students in your class always laugh and smile at school. They are excited to come to school. What do you think makes students happy at school?
- Scenario 4: You have homework every night. You wonder why you have to learn all this stuff. What could you do to make your homework more interesting to you? What has been your favorite homework assignment?
- Scenario 5: Recently, the student council decided that they are going to work on a project where they make school more fun. The principal said the fun still has to be

> **Common Core:**
> CCSS.ELA-LITERACY.SL.1.1.B Build on others' talk in conversations by responding to the comments of others through multiple exchanges.
>
> CCSS.ELA-LITERACY.SL.K-2.1 Participate in collaborative conversations with diverse partners about *grade K, 1, 2 topics and texts* with peers and adults in small and larger groups.
>
> CCSS.ELA-LITERACY.W.K.2 Use a combination of drawing, dictating, and writing to compose informative/explanatory texts in which they name what they are writing about and supply some information about the topic.
>
> **21st Century Skills:**
> Communication, Collaboration, Creativity and Innovation, Critical Thinking and Problem Solving
>
> **ISTE/NETS:**
> Communication and collaboration A, B
>
> Critical thinking, problem solving, and decision making D

connected to learning. What activities could you suggest to the student council that brings more fun to school and help students learn?

Personal Reflection:

Have students pick one of their scenario responses. Invite students to make a star next to this scenario and draw a picture illustrating the scenario.

Group Reflection:

Talk through each scenario. Invite students to present their drawing or writing when it is their turn. Invite an open discussion and feedback from the other students.

Extended Learning:

Create a podcast on Fun & Excitement in GarageBand, iMovie, or another app of your choice. Interview your students about Fun & Excitement. What do they like to learn about and why? What makes school fun for them? Why do they think it's important to enjoy school? What does it feel like to them to be excited about learning? What can they do to be more interested in school? Work with students to add sound effects and music to add excitement to the podcast.

Notes:

Name _____

Draw a picture or write your response in the right hand column.

Some of your friends always complain that school is boring. You enjoy school and have fun learning new things. How can you help your friends enjoy school more? What makes school fun for you?	
Your teacher assigns a project where you can learn and explore anything that interests you. What would you pick?	
Some students in your class always laugh and smile at school. They are excited to come to school. What do you think makes students happy at school?	
You have homework every night. You wonder why you have to learn all this stuff. What could you do to make your homework more interesting to you? What has been your favorite homework assignment?	
Recently, the student council decided that they are going to work on a project where they make school more fun. The principal said the fun still has to be connected to learning. What activities could you suggest to the student council that brings more fun to school and help students learn?	

Grades K-2: Fun & Excitement Activities

Acting It Out

(ABOUT 30 MINUTES)

Common Core:
CCSS.ELA-LITERACY.SL.1.1.B Build on others' talk in conversations by responding to the comments of others through multiple exchanges.

CCSS.ELA-LITERACY.SL.K-2.1 Participate in collaborative conversations with diverse partners about *grade K, 1, 2 topics and texts* with peers and adults in small and larger groups.

CCSS.ELA-LITERACY.RF.K.2.A Recognize and produce rhyming words.

21st Century Skills:
Creativity and Innovation, Communication

ISTE/NETS:
Communication and collaborations B

Creativity and innovation B

Fun & Excitement:
Enjoying what you are doing whether at work, school, or play. Engaging students is the key to Fun & Excitement. Students learn better and enjoy learning more when they are actively involved in whatever they are learning.

Objective:
Students will be able to act out key concepts and understand the purpose of having fun while learning.

Materials:
Note cards, pens or pencils; book of your choice.

Steps:
- Warm-up discussion: Why is it important to be fully into learning when you are at school? Can having fun help you learn?
- Identify action words from a book that you will read to the class. Write these down on note cards.
- Give students three blank note cards. Ask students to write down one word per card. The words on each card can be class related, have a rhyme, or be silly, challenging, or unusual.
- Collect the student cards and mix them with the vocabulary words.
- Tell students that you will read the word on the cards, but that they must stand completely frozen until you say "ACTION." At that point students should act out the word using physical movement, words, dance, for example. After twenty seconds or so, say "END SCENE."
- Continue through the note cards.
- Next, read the story. Ask students to stay still and listen carefully. When you come across one of the selected words say "ACTION" and have students act it out. When you say "END SCENE," students will go back to listening to the story.

Personal Reflection:

Have students complete an exit slip about Fun & Excitement in learning.

- Ask: Why is it important to be fully into what you are learning?
- Did acting the words out help you learn? Why or why not?

Group Reflection:

- Besides acting, what can you do to be fully into learning?
- What activities help you learn best?
- As a class, brainstorm a new strategy that you will use in your next unit.

Extended Learning:

Read a story and have students read stories using different voices and accents.

Super Secret Review: Have students huddle up together and whisper for a review of material. This will build excitement and students will tune in.

Play Character Charades. Act out different characters from a story without speaking.

Rhyme Time: Have students create a beat or download a beat to play. Students will take turns naming different rhyming words to the beat!

Tell stories through dance.

Act out a word problem.

Plan an experiential exercise. For example, when you are teaching about the *Mayflower*, tape out the shape and the size of the boat in a space that is big enough. Learn about the *Mayflower* as students huddle together in the crammed ship.

Notes:
___
___
___
___
___

Grades K-2: Fun & Excitement Activities

Digital Story Telling

(40–50 MINUTES)

Common Core:
CCSS.ELA-LITERACY.RL.1.3
Describe characters, settings, and major events in a story, using key details.

CCSS.ELA-LITERACY.W.2.3
Write narratives in which they recount a well-elaborated event or short sequence of events, include details to describe actions, thoughts, and feelings, use temporal words to signal event order, and provide a sense of closure.

CCSS.ELA-LITERACY.W.K-2.6
With guidance and support from adults, explore a variety of digital tools to produce and publish writing, including in collaboration with peers.

21st Century Skills:
Creativity and Innovation, Media Literacy, Communication, Collaboration

ISTE/NETS:
Creativity and innovation A, B
Communication and collaboration A, B

Fun & Excitement:

Enjoying what you are doing whether at work, school, or play. Engaging students is the key to Fun & Excitement. Students learn better and enjoy learning more when they are actively involved in whatever they are learning.

Objective:

Students will be able to create a digital story.

Materials:

Toontastic app on all devices; iPad or tablet for every three students.

Steps:

- Based on your unit of study, identify several key words or concepts. Post words and concepts on the board.
- Have students work in groups of three to create an original story using these concepts and words.
- Instruct students to open Toontastic app. Click Create Cartoon, then New Cartoon. Next, students will see a story arc. Students should click the paintbrush to design the setup, conflict, challenge, climax, and resolution.
- Have students select a setting or draw their own. They can then click the arrow and select their toys and characters for the story.
- Students can allow Toontastic to access the microphone. When they click start, the app will countdown and then begin recording. They can touch the screen to move the characters around and speak to tell the story. Encourage them to add music and go to the next scene.
- Students should continue to develop each scene. When finished, they can click Done in the upper right hand corner. Have students add a movie title and their names!
- Have students watch their stories by projecting through a projector or Apple TV.

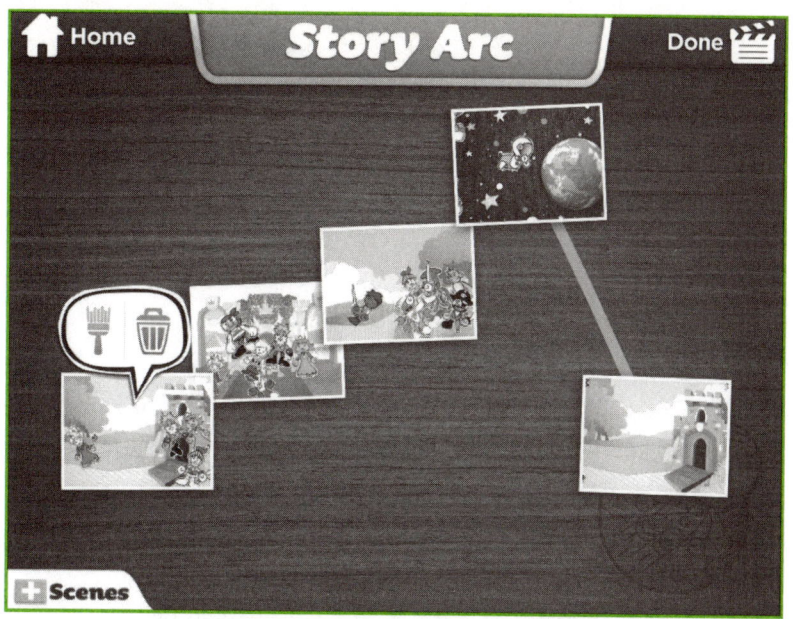

Source: Courtesy of Toontastic.

Personal Reflection:

- What made your story unique?
- What did you enjoy about this activity? How did it help you learn?
- What was it like creating a story with your classmates?

Group Reflection:

Note that even given the same words, our stories were very different. Have students recognize some of the similarities and differences between the stories. Review the key words using different examples from students' stories.

Extended Learning:

Assign each student one of the words from the list. Invite students to become the teacher of that particular word. Students can use the Educreations app to explain the word. Students can write the word using the textbook or marker feature. Next, they can record their voice explaining what the word means. They can also upload a picture from their camera roll or the Web.

Notes:
___
___

CHAPTER 5

Curiosity & Creativity

At the beginning of every new science unit, the third-grade teacher projects an image of an object that has been photographed extremely close up. The object is related to the upcoming content. Students are asked to write down a hypothesis or guess of what the object is on a note card. The teacher collects the note cards and does a quick frequency count by placing similar guesses in the same pile. After learning what the top two or three hypotheses are, the teacher asks students who did *not* have one of these guesses to consider what the students who did have these guesses saw in the photo to make them think that. The students who did have these hypotheses can participate, but only by asking questions. After a few minutes the teacher reveals the answer and begins the unit.

Curious students ask "Why?" Creative students ask "Why not?" While this may oversimplify two very complex realities, curiosity and creativity are paid far too little attention in schools given their importance to lifelong learning and successful living. Despite the number of educators, business people, and politicians that are beating the drum for students to become inquisitive and innovative, to have probing and flexible minds, the educational landscape is still dominated by a common core, common standards, common curricula, and common assessments.

Curiosity & Creativity is about intellectual engagement. Specifically, both curiosity and creativity are products of an engaged imagination. The ability to wonder—in a way that leads to questions and creations—may be a uniquely human capacity. It is the driving force behind both science and art. It is the impulse behind understanding and invention. When students are able to relate what they are learning to material they have previously learned, to other subjects, and to the world around them they become more engaged. When they can use their inborn desire to be creative to develop new ways of thinking and doing they become absorbed in whatever it is they are working on.

No one doubts the critical importance of teaching students to ask and pursue good questions. And very few people (though some do) argue about the importance of teaching students to be original, creative, and innovative. Yet classes that encourage creativity like art and music are cut or shortened to make room for so called "core" subjects. And within those core subjects themselves, student inquiry and questioning is fairly limited by the dictates of the curriculum and what will be on the test. In our work at the Quaglia Institute for Student Aspirations (QISA), we have talked with students who as early as middle school are craving electives that would allow them to pursue their interests and curiosities. How sad is it that in the 2014 national results for the Student Voice Survey, 78% of sixth graders agree with the statement "At school I am encouraged to be creative," but by twelfth grade, just 62% of students agree with that same statement?

The following activities are intended to reverse this trend by helping teachers and students tap their sense of wonder. The exercises invite you to stretch your imagination to become more inquisitive and inventive. The routine of school sometimes can lead to a same-old-same-old dulling of the ability to question and create. By engaging in these playful experiences of Curiosity & Creativity, you will help your students develop habits that support their learning for a lifetime.

Grades 6-8: Curiosity & Creativity Activities

Quick Question

(25 MINUTES)

Common Core:
CCSS.ELA-LITERACY.W.6-8.10
Write routinely over extended time frames (time for research, reflection, and revision) and shorter time frames (a single sitting or a day or two) for a range of discipline-specific tasks, purposes, and audiences.

21st Century Skills:
Creativity and Innovation, Critical Thinking and Problem Solving

ISTE/NETS:
Creativity and innovation A
Critical thinking, problem solving, and decision making D

Curiosity & Creativity:

Asking "Why?" and "Why not?" about the world around you. Curiosity & Creativity encourages students to challenge themselves, ask questions, and think about many different solutions. Creative students approach problems with unique strategies and perspectives. This activity engages students by challenging them to think creatively.

Objective:

Students will be able to formulate unique questions that match a named answer as a critical thinking exercise.

Materials:

Whiteboard and marker; Wordsalad app; random word generator.

Steps:

- Write a list of random words on the board, for example, *yellow, twelve months*, and *Paris*. Use a random word generator. One is available at http://creativitygames.net/random-word-generator/randomwords/1.
- In pairs, ask students to develop several questions that match the answers.
  - The questions for *yellow* might be: What color makes you think of summer? What would be a great name for a golden retriever? What color rhymes with mellow?
  - The questions for *twelve months* might be: How long does a bad week feel? What is the longest time it has taken you to read a book? What was your favorite age? How many months ago did you go on a field trip?
  - The questions for *Paris* might be: Where are you going on vacation? What is Nicky Hilton's older sister's name? What is the City of Lights? Where did you first hear French?
- Challenge pairs to come up with creative and fun questions. Do several rounds of this activity.

Source: Created using Wordsalad.

- Students can use the Wordsalad app to make a word cloud of their creative question. Click the plus sign and start entering words. To keep a sentence together, use the _ key.
- Next, let each pair lead the activity by writing three new words on the board.

Personal Reflection:

- Was it difficult to think differently with this assignment?
- What questions were you most proud of?

Group Reflection:

- Why can thinking of creative questions or answers be challenging?
- Why do you think it is difficult for students to ask questions?
- What are some ways we can practice thinking differently?

Extended Learning:

Students should pick a topic or class concept that interests them. Ask students to research that topic and display their information in a creative way while sharing facts and images. Students can create a Popplet mind map. Encourage students to think differently while creating their Popplet. Students may show connections, relationships between concepts, link questions and answers, for example. Check out the Popplet YouTube video for an overview of how to use this app at https://www.youtube.com/watch?v=CxLDsWHsQ1g.

Grades 6-8: Curiosity & Creativity Activities

The Curiosity Convention

(TO BE DETERMINED BY TEACHER/SEVERAL CLASS PERIODS)

Common Core:
CCSS.ELA-LITERACY.WHST.6-8.7
Conduct short as well as more sustained research projects to answer a question (including a self-generated question) or solve a problem; narrow or broaden the inquiry when appropriate; synthesize multiple sources on the subject, demonstrating understanding of the subject under investigation.

21st Century Skills:
Critical Thinking and Problem Solving, Creativity and Innovation, Collaboration, Initiative and Self-Direction, Productivity and Accountability

ISTE/NETS:
Creativity and innovation B
Communication and collaboration A
Research and information fluency B, C, D
Critical thinking, problem solving, and decision making A, B, C, D

Curiosity & Creativity:

Asking "Why?" and "Why not?" about the world around you. Students will independently explore and research what they are curious about and share their findings.

Objective:

Students will be able to form an inquiry-based question, organize research, compose a presentation, and share findings about a topic they are curious about.

Materials:

Paper; technology for researching; individual materials may vary depending on project.

Steps:

- Present an invitation to the class: You are invited to present at the Curiosity Convention. Inform students that they are going to have the opportunity to learn and share about anything they want!
- Allow students to brainstorm a list of things they are curious about. Have students partner and share some of their answers. Next, share some ideas with the whole class.
- Explain that students will have an opportunity to dig deeper and explore one of their curiosities. Students will need to form an inquiry-based question.
- Give students time to research their projects.
- Have students create a presentation to share their findings at the Curiosity Convention. Encourage students to present their information in a creative way to engage their audience.
- Prep for the Curiosity Convention! Have students create posters and signs in the spirit of curiosity. Option: Invite other classes or adults to join in on the learning fun by attending the convention as observers.

Personal Reflection:

- What was it like to research, explore, and present on what you are curious about?
- Why can it be more interesting to explore your own questions rather than questions that teachers assign?
- How would you rate your engagement in this project?

Group Reflection:

- Share the following quote from Angela Maiers: "You are a genius. The world expects your contribution." Ask students: What are you teaching the world? How did your projects help teach the world? What did you learn from your classmates? Watch the video *Kid President's Pep Talk to Teachers and Students!* at https://www.youtube.com/watch?v=RwlhUcSGqgs.
- Discuss the following quote from Albert Einstein: "It is a miracle that curiosity survives formal education." Allow students time to reflect, give examples, and provide a rationale if they agree or disagree with this quote.

Extended Learning:

Have students create a curiosity journal or begin a notes section on a personal device. Students may use Note Taker HD or another note-taking app. Students will write down questions and ideas that they are curious about. When they are bored, encourage students to begin to answer those questions.

Notes:

_____
_____
_____
_____
_____
_____
_____

Grades 6-8: Curiosity & Creativity Activities

Marshmallow Challenge

(ABOUT 50 MINUTES)

Common Core:
CCSS.ELA-LITERACY.SL.6-8.1 Engage effectively in a range of collaborative discussions (one-on-one, in groups, and teacher-led) with diverse partners on grade 6-8 topics, texts, and issues, building on others' ideas and expressing their own clearly.

21st Century Skills:
Critical Thinking and Problem Solving, Creativity and Innovation, Collaboration

ISTE/NETS:
Creativity and innovation A
Communication and collaboration D
Critical thinking, problem solving, and decision making B

Curiosity & Creativity:

Asking "Why?" and "Why not?" about the world around you. Students will use creative thinking skills to build a tall structure out of uncooked spaghetti, string, marshmallow, and tape.

Objective:

Students will be able to use creative thinking skills and collaborate with peers to build a structure out of random objects.

Materials:

A marshmallow challenge kit for each team: twenty sticks of spaghetti, one yard of masking tape, one yard of string and one marshmallow. These ingredients should be placed into a paper lunch bag.

Steps:

- Prior to the activity, have students go to http://marshmallowchallenge.com/Instructions.html for step-by-step instructions on set up, directions, and more helpful hints.
- Form groups of four students.
- Begin the challenge.
- To debrief, show this video: http://www.ted.com/talks/tom_wujec_build_a_tower.

Personal Reflection:

- How did you use creative thinking during this exercise?
- Describe a real-life situation where you used creative thinking.
- How did your team collaborate?
- Describe a real-life situation where you collaborated.

Group Reflection:

- What skills did you use during the marshmallow challenge?
- What roles did everyone take on?
- Why is having diverse skills important?
- How did the different structures vary?

Extended Learning:

Students should use their curiosity and creative thinking skills as they take apart a toy and create a new, unique invention. Students will bring in a toy they no longer play with and dissect their doll, remote control airplane, or plush toy. Next, students should use the parts to create a new, unique toy. Visit http://tinkering.exploratorium.edu/toy-take-apart.

Notes:

Grades 3-5: Curiosity & Creativity Activities

Genius Gallery

(TO BE DETERMINED BY TEACHER/SEVERAL CLASS PERIODS)

Common Core:
CCSS.ELA-LITERACY.W.3-5.7
Conduct short research projects that use several sources to build knowledge through investigation of different aspects of a topic.

CCSS.ELA-LITERACY.W.5.9
Draw evidence from literary or informational texts to support analysis, reflection, and research.

21st Century Skills:
Critical Thinking and Problem Solving, Creativity and Innovation, Collaboration, Initiative and Self-Direction, Productivity and Accountability

ISTE/NETS:
Creativity and innovation B
Communication and collaboration A,
Research and information fluency B, C, D
Critical thinking, problem solving, and decision making A, B, C, D

Curiosity & Creativity:

Asking "Why?" and "Why not?" about the world around you. Students will independently explore and research what they are curious about and share their findings.

Objective:

Students will be able to form an inquiry-based question, research, and share findings about a topic they are curious about.

Materials:

Paper; technology for researching; individual materials may vary depending on project.

Steps:

- Before the lesson, watch the *Genius Hour* video for inspiration at http://www.geniushour.com.
- Present an invitation to the class: You are to attend and present at the Genius Gallery. Inform students that they are going to have the opportunity to learn and share about anything they want!
- Allow students to brainstorm a list of things they are curious about. Have students partner up and share some of their answers. Next, share some ideas with the whole class.
- Explain that students will have an opportunity to dig deeper and explore one of their curiosities. Students will need to form an inquiry-based question.
- Give students time to research their inquiry-based question. Along the way, have students reflect on their achievement on each session they have to work on their Genius Gallery project.
- Students should create a presentation to share their findings to their question at the Genius Gallery. Encourage students to present their information in a creative way to engage their audience.

- Prep for the Genius Gallery! Have students create posters and signs in the spirit of curiosity. Option: Invite other classes and adults to attend the gallery to join in on the learning fun!

Personal Reflection:

- What was it like to research, explore, and present on what you are curious about?
- Why can it be more interesting to explore your own questions rather than questions that teachers assign?
- How would you rate your engagement in this project?

Group Reflection:

Share the following quote from Angela Maiers: "You are a genius. The world expects your contribution." Ask: What are you teaching the world? How did your projects help teach the world? What did you learn from your classmates? Watch the *Kid President's Pep Talk to Teachers and Students!* video at https://www.youtube.com/watch?v=RwlhUcSGqgs.

Extended Learning:

Have students create a curiosity journal or begin a notes section on a personal device. Students should write down questions and ideas that they are curious about. When they are bored, encourage students to begin to answer those questions.

Notes:

_____
_____
_____
_____
_____
_____
_____

Grades 3-5: Curiosity & Creativity Activities

Mystery Picture

(15 MINUTES PER DAY FOR FOUR TO FIVE DAYS; 20 MINUTE FOLLOW-UP)

Common Core:
CCSS.ELA-LITERACY.W.3-5.7
Conduct short research projects that use several sources to build knowledge through investigation of different aspects of a topic.

CCSS.ELA-LITERACY.SL 3-5.1
Engage effectively in a range of collaborative discussion

21st Century Skills:
Creativity and Innovation, Collaboration, Media Literacy, Critical Thinking and Problem Solving

ISTE/NETS:
Research and informational fluency A

Curiosity & Creativity:

Asking "Why?" and "Why not?" about the world around you. Curiosity & Creativity encourages students to use their imaginations and broaden their views. This activity engages students and invites them to think creatively.

Objective:

Students will be able to inspect a "mystery picture" and theorize on what it could be.

Materials:

Pictures of food, animals, objects that you will progressively zoom in on or zoom out.

Steps:

- Inform students that you are going to present a mystery picture to the class at the beginning of the week. You will need to create or download an extremely close up or far away picture ahead of time.
- You will show the picture to the students for one minute for a period of four or five days.
- Each day, ask students to write down their guesses about what the picture is. Students should explain their guesses. You should provide a clue about the mystery picture. For example, on one day the clue might be that the picture is of a living thing and on day two the clue might be that the picture is of a mammal.
- Share the original picture on the last day of the week. Encourage students to research the subject of the picture.
- After students understand the process, allow students to pick out a mystery picture and lead the activity.

Personal Reflection:

- How did this activity spark your curiosity?
- What are you curious about learning?

Group Reflection:

As a class, brainstorm action steps that students can take to increase their curiosity and creativity. Examples can be to

- explore the outdoors;
- write a poem or short story just for fun;
- take an interesting photograph;
- ask ten questions every day this week;
- find a new app that allows you to be creative;
- build a fort;
- write a song;
- challenge yourself to ask more questions; or
- with an adult, discover how something mechanical works.

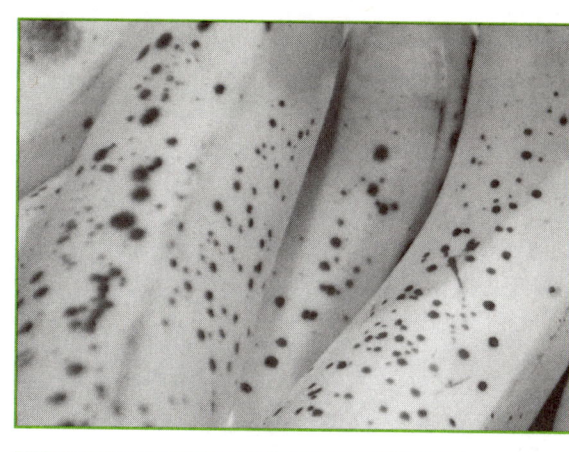

Source: © moodboard/Thinkstock Photos

Extended Learning:

Have students create a picture collage that expresses curiosity. Include pictures of things you wonder about. Use PicCollage, Pic Stitch, or another photo app. If technology is not available, have students create a paper picture collage using such items as paper or magazines.

Notes:
_____
_____
_____
_____
_____
_____

Grades 3-5: Curiosity & Creativity Activities

Invention Convention

(SEVERAL CLASS PERIODS)

Common Core:
CCSS.ELA-LITERACY.W.3-5.7
Conduct short research projects that use several sources to build knowledge through investigation of different aspects of a topic.
CCSS.ELA-LITERACY.SL 3-5.1
Engage effectively in a range of collaborative discussion.

21st Century Skills:
Creativity and Innovation, Critical Thinking and Problem Solving, Flexibility and Adaptability

ISTE/NETS:
Creativity and innovation A, C, D
Communication and collaboration B
Research and information fluency A, B, C, D
Critical thinking, problem solving, and decision making A, B, C, D

Curiosity & Creativity:
Asking "Why?" and "Why not?" about the world around you.

Objective:
Students will be able to identify an everyday problem to solve. Students will be able to develop a creative solution.

Materials:
Research materials; materials will vary for each project.

Steps:

- Students should identify problems they would like to solve. Guide students by asking: What problems would you like to see solved? What does not work as well as you would like it to? What could help you at home? School? Hygiene? Taking care of your pet? Doing your homework? The mall? Park? Movies? Traveling?
- Have each student focus on one of the problems they identified.
- Instruct students to find relevant research on the problem.
- Have them brainstorm solutions.
- Students should then develop an invention or invention model that solves the problem.
- Ask students to test their inventions and make improvements.
- Students should use the scientific method, develop a report, create visual aids, and prepare for a presentation.

Invite students to present their invention to the class or school at an event called the Invention Convention. Each student should present his or her findings, show an example, and answer questions about the invention.

Personal Reflection:

- What was the name of your invention?
- What are you most proud of about your invention?
- What did you learn through the inventing process that was most meaningful to you?

Group Reflection:

- What inventions did you find interesting?
- What does it feel like to invent something?
- Why is it important to use your imagination when inventing?
- How can we use our imagination and creative thinking at school more often?

Sample Rubric:

Did student clearly identify a problem?

Did student organize relevant research on the problem?

Did student develop an invention or model that would help solve the problem?

Did the student present the information in a clear fashion?

Did the student use visual aids?

Was the scientific method used?

Extended Learning:

Watch *"Shark Tank" Young Entrepreneurs* video clip at https://www.youtube.com/watch?v=qF-ShW-qxPM4. Explain that inventors have to be able to articulate their ideas and pitch them to investors or customers. Have students develop a business pitch to convince others that their invention is the best! Invite them to tell a story about their product, share data and information, and be personable. Students should deliver their pitch to the class. Give students play money and have them choose which product they would invest their money in and explain why they think the invention would be successful!

Check out other inventor related lesson plans and resources at http://www.just-think-inc.com/documents/LessonGuide2012.pdf.

Notes:
_____
_____
_____

Grades K-2: Curiosity & Creativity Activities

What's in the Bag?

(20–30 MINUTES)

Common Core:
CCSS.ELA-LITERACY.W.K.3
Use a combination of drawing, dictating, and writing to narrate a single event or several loosely linked events, tell about the events in the order in which they occurred, and provide a reaction to what happened.

CCSS.ELA-LITERACY.W.1.3
Write narratives in which they recount two or more appropriately sequenced events, include some details regarding what happened, use temporal words to signal event order, and provide some sense of closure.

CCSS.ELA-LITERACY.W.2.3
Write narratives in which they recount a well-elaborated event or short sequence of events, include details to describe actions, thoughts, and feelings, use temporal words to signal event order, and provide a sense of closure.

21st Century Skills:
Creativity and Innovation

ISTE/NETS:
Creativity and innovation A

Curiosity & Creativity:

Asking "Why?" and "Why not?" about the world around you. Curiosity is about helping students to wonder and think differently. This activity encourages students to be curious and then creative with their answers.

Objective:

Students will be able to create a unique, imaginative hypothesis from touching an object in a bag.

Materials:

Brown lunch bags; random assortment of fun items to put in the bags—pencils, moss, popcorn—get creative.

Steps:

- Before the activity, put a variety of items in ten different brown paper bags. Label bags 1 to 10.
- Let students know they are going to guess what is in the bag, but they are free to use their imaginations with the guesses. For example, a bag with a pencil might be a magic wand that makes recess last twice as long.
- Encourage students to shake the bags, to feel inside, but tell them they cannot look inside the bags.
- Have students label a piece of paper 1 to 10, so they can match their responses with the correct bag.
- Have students share answers and acknowledge the creative guesses!

Personal Reflection:

- What was it like to use your imagination to answer the questions?
- What object were you most curious about? Why?
- Research one of the objects and record a fact that you found interesting.

Group Reflection:
- Why is it important to wonder about the world around us?
- What are you curious about?

Extended Learning:
Invite students to draw, write, and tell a story about one of their creative guesses using Educreations Interactive Whiteboard app. Students can record their voices and add photos and drawings.

Notes:
_____
_____
_____
_____
_____
_____
_____
_____
_____
_____
_____
_____
_____
_____
_____

Grades K-2: Curiosity & Creativity Activities

Surroundings Scavenger Hunt

(40–50 MINUTES)

Common Core:
CCSS.ELA-LITERACY.W.K-1.8
With guidance and support from adults, recall information from experiences or gather information from provided sources to answer a question.

CCSS.ELA-LITERACY.W.2.8
Recall information from experiences or gather information from provided sources to answer a question.

21st Century Skills:
Critical Thinking and Problem Solving, Collaboration

ISTE/NETS:
Research and information fluency D
Creativity and innovation D
Critical thinking, problem solving, and decision making C

Curiosity & Creativity:

Asking "Why?" and "Why not?" about the world around you. Curiosity helps our minds grow and discover wonderful new things.

Objective:

Students will be able to analyze items collected in a nature scavenger hunt.

Materials:

Brown paper bag; scavenger hunt checklist attached to each bag.

Steps:

- The day before the activity, have students do a *K-W-L* chart (what I **K**now, what I **W**ant to know, what I **L**earned) about the plants and natural parts of the world outside of the school. Have students fill out the Know and Want to know columns. Ask students what they know about the natural things around the school and what they want to know.
- From the list, pick different natural items that students would be able to recognize or things that students want to learn about. Create a scavenger hunt checklist. Some examples may include the following: rock, leaf, wildflower, dandelion, berry, stick, green grass, feather, something smooth, something rough, something soft, something square. Encourage students to pick up additional items that interest them. Explain what items are off limits for picking.
- Give each student or small groups of students a brown paper bag with the checklist attached.
- Allow students to gather items from the checklist outside.
- Return to the classroom and have students share their items.
- Compare items, sizes, weights, colors, and shapes. Discuss the items.
- Have students do research about the items they want to learn more about. Fill in this information to the Learn section of the *K-W-L* chart.

Personal Reflection:

- What was the most surprising thing you learned?
- What object were you most curious about? Why?

Group Reflection:

- How does curiosity help our minds grow?
- What did you discover outside?

Extended Learning:

Create a new scavenger hunt list for students to accomplish as they explore the inside of school. This time students will collect pictures of each item. The collection may include a selfie with the school counselor, a picture of the recycling bins, a picture of a friend eating in the cafeteria, or a picture of someone shaking hands with the school secretary.

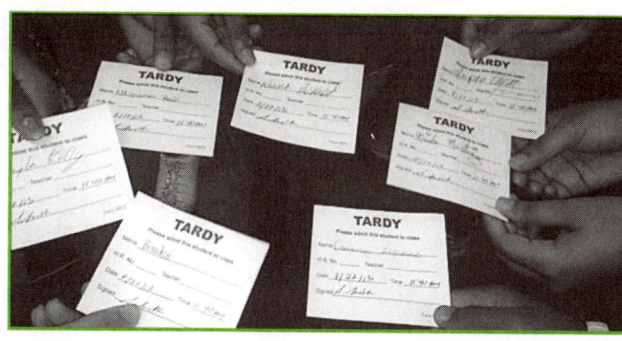

On one school scavenger hunt, students visited the attendance office and received a pretend tardy slip. The secretary also reviewed procedures in case a student will be late or absent!

Source: Photo by Julie Hellerstein.

Notes:

Grades K-2: Curiosity & Creativity Activities

Mad Libs

(ABOUT 30 MINUTES)

Common Core:
CCSS.ELA-LITERACY.RF.1-2.4.C Use context to confirm or self-correct word recognition and understanding, rereading as necessary.

CCSS.ELA-LITERACY.L.K-2.1 Demonstrate command of the conventions of standard English grammar and usage when writing or speaking.

21st Century Skills:
Information Literacy, Creativity and Innovation, Collaboration

ISTE/NETS:
Creativity and innovation D

Communication and collaboration D

Technology operations and concepts A

Curiosity & Creativity:
Asking "Why?" and "Why not?" about the world around you.

Objective:
Students will be able to identify nouns, verbs, and adjectives to create a Mad Libs story.

Materials:
Mad Libs download printable worksheets; Mad Libs app on iPad or device.

Steps:

- Warm-up discussion: Why is it fun to use your imagination when telling a story? What is the most creative story you have told?
- Tell students that today they are going to use different parts of speech to complete a story. Review parts of speech: nouns, adjectives, verbs, and so on. Say: We are going to form a story without knowing much context for the story. Ask: What is context? Why is it important to reread stories to understand the context when you encounter a new word?
- Download the Mad Libs app to an iOS device. Click Play. Select twenty-one free stories. Pick a story. Ask students to provide you with words that match the part of speech requested. For example, it will ask you to type a plural noun. Type the word. You can also click Hints for some examples of plural nouns.
- Continue to fill out the story calling on students for their input.
- Next, have students select an image to go along with their story. Invite students to take a picture of other students or something in your classroom that may relate to the story.
- Click Done.
- Read the story aloud!
- Select the next Mad Lib and repeat the process.

Personal Reflection:

- How are you creative at school?
- What does it feel like to use your imagination?

Group Reflection:

- How would the story be different if we knew the context? Go back and read the story aloud and allow students to edit the words they filled in to make the story become more realistic. Why is it important to sometimes be realistic and sometimes creative?
- Create a list of projects and activities where you have been creative. What would you like to do in this class to help you be more creative?

Extended Learning:

Invite students to create a song, cheer, skit, or picture that goes along to one of the Mad Libs stories.

Students can create their own Mad Libs story. Have students create a short story. Next, ask students to highlight ten words. With a partner, have students look up the word's part of speech. Rewrite the story and leave blanks for the highlighted words. Underneath the blank, write the part of speech. Have students play their story with family or friends not in their class.

Notes:

CHAPTER 6

Spirit of Adventure

Many schools use field trips as a kind of end of the year out-of-school reward for during the year in-school good behavior. But getting out of the school building holds the promise of being so much more than a carrot at the end of a stick for motivating students to behave or work hard. One school figured this out by agreeing as a staff that all field trips must have a stated learning objective and be integrated with the curriculum. Far from limiting field trips, this had the effect of challenging the staff to discover the many ways learning could take place in the community around them. While the local museum and science center remained popular options, trips were planned to the bridal shop to learn about the importance of measuring and planning (as part of a math chapter), the local newspaper to learn about investigative writing and editing (as part of an ELA unit), and a nearby animal shelter to learn about how placement specialists figure out who should adopt a new pet (as part of a social studies chapter). These experiences took students (and teachers) out of the confining comfort of the classroom and the safe routine of worksheets into seeing the challenges of the real world application of what they had previously experienced only in their textbooks.

One of our favorite quotes is from Helen Keller: "Life is either a daring adventure or nothing at all." Out on the very edge of what we are capable of and at the limits of our insights and skills there is a horizon called learning. And it is infinite in scope. That is to say, if we are willing to push ourselves, to move beyond our comfort zones, to take risks, there is no limit to what we can come to understand and know and discover. The adventure of learning is what brought Marco Polo to the East, van Gogh to his canvas, and NASA to the moon. Daring makes it all possible.

Sadly, we have been in schools and talked with students who do not dare to dare. Students tell us they are afraid to answer a question for fear of looking stupid. Others tell us they are afraid to answer a question for fear of looking smart. Some students are afraid to fail, while others are afraid to succeed. "If I do well on a test," one student told us, "they'll expect me to do that well every time." The fact of the matter is, that while we have done well with making it safe to make mistakes, we have not yet made it entirely safe in school to be successful. Despite the future earning potential of nerds and geeks, they are still made fun of in many schools.

The challenge for Spirit of Adventure is the individualized nature of risk-taking behavior. Some people are risk seekers; others are risk averse. Some people will try anything; others prefer the tried and true. We have observed classes where some students are leaping out of their seats to read aloud while others are leaving their seats to go to the restroom in the hopes of not being asked to read aloud. It is one of the trickier parts of being a skilled teacher: knowing when to push a student and when to provide security. But there is no denying that little learning takes place when a student is either panicked or overly comfortable. Learning takes place when students are being challenged.

The exercises in this chapter will help you and your students find that sweet spot. Students will learn what it feels like to challenge themselves beyond their comfort zones, but short of their panic zones. Students will be invited to take risks in the safety of the activity and the fun of trying new experiences together. By taking on the healthy risks created by the exercise, they will learn how learning itself is an adventure.

Grades 6-8: Spirit of Adventure Activities

Student Speak

(50 MINUTES, SPACE OUT STUDENT PRESENTATIONS OVER THE NEXT FEW WEEKS, HAVING ONE OR TWO STUDENTS PRESENT AT A TIME)

Common Core:
CCSS.ELA-LITERACY.SL.6-8.4
Present claims and findings, sequencing ideas logically and using pertinent descriptions, facts, and details to accentuate main ideas or themes; use appropriate eye contact, adequate volume, and clear pronunciation.

CCSS.ELA-LITERACY.SL.6-8.5
Include multimedia components (e.g., graphics, images, music, sound) and visual displays in presentations to clarify information.

21st Century Skills:
Communication, Creativity and Innovation, Initiative and Self-Direction

ISTE/NETS:
Research and information fluency A
Communication and collaboration B

Spirit of Adventure:
Being excited to try new things, even if you don't know if you'll excel. Spirit of Adventure encourages students to take healthy risks. This activity encourages students to take risks by providing them with a safe and comfortable environment to share and teach out of their expertise and interest.

Objective:
Students will be able to report on a topic of their choice.

Materials:
Projector; video clip from Google Nexus TV commercial.

Steps:
- Watch the Google Nexus TV commercial at http://www.ispot.tv/ad/7qCq/google-nexus-7-speech.
- Ask students: What does it feel like to speak in front of the class? Does knowing the subject matter well help you speak in front of the class?
- Discuss how students have varied interests and knowledge and how it is important to share their interests.
- Ask students to make a list of things they are interested in and know a lot about.
- Place no limit on what a student may be good at—video games, gaining Instagram followers, knitting, dancing, knowing where to find clothes on sale, for example.
- Invite students to create a short presentation or demonstration on their interests and expertise. Allow students to bring in props, visual aids, or do something creative for their presentation.
- Allow students to share their expertise over the course of several weeks.

Personal Reflection:

What was it like to talk in front of the class regarding something you were confident about?

Self-Assessment: Students will score themselves on the following statements: Always, Most of the time, Sometimes, Seldom, Never.

1. I have someone to talk to when I feel overwhelmed at school.
2. I try to be successful in all my classes.
3. I set goals for myself.
4. I like being challenged at school.
5. I am not afraid to make mistakes.
6. I want to be successful.
7. I push myself to do better in school.
8. I ask for help when I need it.

Source: Photo by Julie Hellerstein.

Group Reflection:

- Why do you think public speaking is such a big fear for some people? How can we act to reduce this fear?
- Why is it important to speak out and participate in class?
- What are some other common fears?

Extended Learning:

Students will search the Internet and select a public speaking activity for the class to complete. Have the student set up and lead the activity. Here are some examples: http://publicspeakingpower.com/fun-public-speaking-activities/, http://www.write-out-loud.com/public-speaking-activities.html.

Grades 6-8: Spirit of Adventure Activities

Adventure Advice

(40–50 MINUTES)

Common Core:
CCSS.ELA-LITERACY.W.6-8.2
Write informative/explanatory texts to examine a topic and convey ideas, concepts, and information through the selection, organization, and analysis of relevant content.

CCSS.ELA-LITERACY.W.6-8.6
Use technology, including the Internet, to produce and publish writing and link to and cite sources as well as to interact and collaborate with others, including linking to and citing sources.

21st Century Skills:
Communication, Creativity and Innovation

ISTE/NETS:
Communication and collaboration B
Creativity and innovation A, B,
Digital citizenship B

Spirit of Adventure:

Being excited to try new things, even if you don't know if you'll excel.

Objective:

Students will be able to write an advice column addressing how to overcome fears and include personal experience.

Materials:

Sticky notes.

Steps:

- Ask students to write advice columns about how to have a Spirit of Adventure and overcome fears.
- Prewrite: Identify a time you were afraid to try something new. What did it feel like to be afraid? What were you afraid of at the time? Remind students to keep these feelings in mind for this assignment.
- Invite students to write down what they are afraid to do both in school and life on a sticky note and post it on the board. Examples can be public speaking, singing in front of a group, striking out at a baseball game, or failing a test.
- Next, have students look at the sticky notes and select a fear that they could give good advice about.
- Students should then write a digital advice column to their peers about their experience overcoming that fear. The student should include advice and different strategies to try. Students should include multimedia images, GIFs, videos, or relevant resource links.
- Compile all the articles into a newsletter.

Personal Reflection:

- What was it like using your personal experience to help someone else?
- How many of the fears could you relate to?
- What skills or coping strategies are most useful to you when trying something new?

Group Reflection:

Share articles. Have students discuss the articles in pairs. As a whole group, create a list of strategies and tools for overcoming fears.

Extended Learning:

Have students create a Pinterest board of things they would like to try. They should include motivational quotes about having a Spirit of Adventure. Students can work with a peer and invite him or her to work on their board by clicking add people to the board.

Notes:

Grades 6-8: Spirit of Adventure Activities

Never Lose Sight of Your Goal

(ABOUT 30 MINUTES)

Common Core:
CCSS.ELA-LITERACY.W.6-8.2
Write informative/explanatory texts to examine a topic and convey ideas, concepts, and information through the selection, organization, and analysis of relevant content.

CCSS.ELA-LITERACY.W.6-8.6
Use technology, including the Internet, to produce and publish writing and link to and cite sources as well as to interact and collaborate with others, including linking to and citing sources.

21st Century Skills:
Creativity and Innovation, Initiative and Self-Direction, Productivity and Accountability

ISTE/NETS:
Creativity and innovation B
Communication and collaboration B

Spirit of Adventure:

Being excited to try new things, even if you don't know if you'll excel. Spirit of Adventure is about setting and achieving goals. This activity encourages students to choose goals that are important to them and work toward achieving their goals.

Objective:

Students will identify a meaningful goal and create a visual representation of their goal.

Materials:

Note cards, pens and pencils; devices; and photo-editing apps.

Steps:

- Warm-up discussion: What has been your experience with goal setting? What is a goal you have recently achieved? How did you stay focused on your goal?
- Discuss some of your own personal or professional goals. Share some strategies on how not to lose sight of your goals.
- Students should set one measurable, realistic, and meaningful goal that they can achieve in the next two weeks to a month.
- Students should create a visual representation of their goal. As a challenge, have students keep this visual representation in their "sight." For example, have students write and draw their goal on a note card and have them fold it up and tie their shoelaces over the top. Students could create a new phone background representing their goal. Students can create an accessory to wear.

Personal Reflection:

- Explain your goal and visualization of your goal.
- Identify three steps that you need to take to achieve your goal.
- Identify someone who can help you achieve the goal.
- How will you evaluate your success in reaching this goal? In this activity, you identified a short-term goal. What is your long-term goal?

Group Reflection:

- In small groups, students should present their visual representations of their goals. Have them discuss why it is important to never lose sight of their goals.
- Invite students to discuss if they have ever revised and changed their goals. Why is this important?

Extended Learning:

Ask students to create a multimedia presentation about the challenges they have conquered since they have started school. For example, maybe in first grade they had a challenging time learning to read or making friends. Next, students should think about what challenges they might face in high school. What themes do they see in all their challenges? What type of support do they think they will need to tackle future challenges?

Source: Photo by Julie Hellerstein.

Notes:
___
___
___
___
___
___
___

Grades 3-5: Spirit of Adventure Activities

Support Me Selfie

(30–40 MINUTES)

Common Core:
CCSS.ELA-LITERACY.SL 3-5.1 Engage effectively in a range of collaborative discussion

CCSS.ELA-LITERACY.W.3-5.10 Write routinely over extended time frames (time for research, reflection, and revision) and shorter time frames (a single sitting or a day or two) for a range of discipline-specific tasks, purposes, and audiences.

21st Century Skills:
Collaboration, Creativity and Innovation

ISTE/NETS:
Communication and collaboration B, D

Creativity and innovation B

Spirit of Adventure:

Being excited to try new things, even if you don't know if you'll excel. Spirit of Adventure is about creating an environment where it's okay for students to take healthy risks. This activity gives students a chance to feel safer taking risks!

Objective:

Students will be able to identify a skill or area where they need support. Students will be able to write a short personal narrative about a time when they did not receive support.

Materials:

Posters, markers; camera.

Steps:

- Warm-up discussion: What does it feel like to be laughed at when you make a mistake? How can we be more supportive of one another in class as we learn?
- Share a personal story about a time when you were laughed at for making a mistake.
- Invite students to share about a time when they were laughed at for making a mistake.
- Students should then share about a time when they felt support from someone when they made a mistake.
- Ask: How can students show support for each other? Cheering? Smiling? Showing respect? Being patient? Encouraging? Giving advice?
- Have each student identify something that they want to improve upon. Ask students to make a "Support Me" poster. Examples: "Support me when I don't know the answer." "Support me when I try to learn Spanish."
- Have students hold up their posters and take a "selfie" of each student. Then, take a group picture of the class holding up their posters. Hang the picture in your room or make it your computer background.

Personal Reflection:

Students will write a short narrative about a time when they were laughed at for making a mistake. Alternatively, students will write about a time when they felt support from someone when they made a mistake. Encourage students to use a graphic organizer to set up their story. One is available at http://www.scholastic.com/teachers/top-teaching/2014/03/graphic-organizers-personal-narratives.

Group Reflection:

When have you showed someone else support as they were learning or trying something new? Give examples in a shared Google document or list on the board. Have students add to the list as they show each other support.

Extended Learning:

Show the *From Failing You Learn, Keep Moving Forward* video clip from *Meet the Robinsons* at https://www.youtube.com/watch?v=7p_eKV3SzwE.

Discuss: Why were the other characters celebrating? Do you learn from mistakes? When have you learned from making a mistake? How did you keep moving forward?

As a class, come up with a cheer, chant, or phrase that shows support when someone has made a mistake while learning or is trying something new.

Have students design a logo or symbol that shows that making mistakes is okay in the learning process. Put this symbol on your class website and on your door. Examples can be seen at http://art-educ4kids.weebly.com/logos-and-design.html.

Notes:

Grades 3-5: Spirit of Adventure Activities

Adventure Action Cards

(10–15 MINUTES, 20 MINUTE FOLLOW-UP SEVERAL DAYS LATER)

Common Core:
CCSS.ELA-LITERACY.W.3-5.10
Write routinely over extended time frames (time for research, reflection, and revision) and shorter time frames (a single sitting or a day or two) for a range of discipline-specific tasks, purposes, and audiences.

CCSS.ELA-LITERACY.SL.3-5.1
Engage effectively in a range of collaborative discussions (one-on-one, in groups, and teacher-led) with diverse partners on *grade 3-5 topics and texts*, building on others' ideas and expressing their own clearly.

21st Century Skills:
Collaboration, Communication, Creativity and Innovation, Media Literacy

ISTE/NETS:
Communication and collaboration A
Creativity and innovation B

Spirit of Adventure:
Being excited to try new things, even if you don't know if you'll excel.

Objective:
Students will be able to accept and reflect on a challenge that requires a Spirit of Adventure.

Materials:
Sticky notes for every student; Microsoft Word or a tech tool to make a list with pictures and writing.

Steps:

- Warm-up discussion: Why is it important to have a Spirit of Adventure in life and school?
- Explain to students that they are going to dare each other to have a Spirit of Adventure. Students should write Adventure Actions on sticky notes and post them on the board. Feel free to use the following examples.
    - Read a book from a new genre. For example, if nonfiction is your thing, try a mystery novel.
    - Order something unique off the menu at a restaurant.
    - Play a new game at recess.
    - Use a new type of technology.
    - Sit with a new friend.
    - Ask a question in class.
    - Try a new type of art project.
    - Wear a unique outfit to school.
    - Ask someone new to be your partner on a project.
    - Share a talent with your teachers.

- - Join a new club.
  - Enter a competition that you may not be good at.
  - Take part in a dance-off.
  - Eat something unusual.
- Be sure all the challenges are safe.
- Allow students to go up to the board and accept an Adventure Action card.
- Have students read their Adventure Action card aloud. Allow students to give advice, feedback, or tell relevant stories about the actions.

Personal Reflection:

Take a picture of you completing your Adventure Action card. Describe what Adventure Action you picked.

- What did you do? How did you feel while doing the activity?
- What was the most difficult part of this task?
- What did this experience teach you?

Group Reflection:

- Students will display and share pictures.
- How can having a Spirit of Adventure help you in school and other real-life situations?
- How has your thinking changed as a result of this assignment?
- Create an adventure action challenge for the whole class to do together. Here are some examples: Create a parody to a popular song around a classroom concept, learn advanced words in Spanish, or perform a play for another class.

Extended Learning:

Have each student create a personalized bucket list. Encourage students to be creative with the format, colors, and pictures of the bucket list. The bucket list should include twenty to thirty statements that they will need a Spirit of Adventure to complete. PictCheck is an app where students can create a list and add pictures. They can also check boxes off as they complete their bucket list.

Notes:
_____
_____
_____

Grades 3-5: Spirit of Adventure Activities

Bull's-Eye

(20–30 MINUTES)

Common Core:
CCSS.ELA-LITERACY.W.4.10
Write routinely over extended time frames (time for research, reflection, and revision) and shorter time frames (a single sitting or a day or two) for a range of discipline-specific tasks, purposes, and audiences.

21st Century Skills:
Initiative and Self-Direction, Flexibility and Adaptability

ISTE/NETS:
Creativity and innovation B

Spirit of Adventure:

Being excited to try new things, even if you don't know if you'll excel. Spirit of Adventure is about setting positive goals with students, not for students. This activity introduces students to goal setting in a fun and engaging way.

Objective:

Students will identify steps they need to take in order to reach their goals.

Materials:

Bull's-Eye Goal Setting Sheet; stickers for students as they reach their goals.

Steps:

- Warm-up discussion: What does it mean to set a goal for yourself? Why is it important to set goals?
- Ask students to identify something they would like to do better in the next few weeks.
- As a class, brainstorm several goals. Goals should be obtainable and measurable. Let students know they are going to set a goal for themselves.
- After students have decided on a goal, hand out a bull's-eye graphic organizer.
- Students should write their goal in the space provided and place a sticker outside of the circle.
- Then students should write the steps they need to take to attain their goal, starting with Step 1 in the outside circle.
- As students complete each step, give students a sticker to place in the circle. Once their goal is complete, let students color the center bull's-eye. Students should monitor their own progress.
- Celebrate as students accomplish their goals. Help others revise, rewrite, or create new goals if necessary.

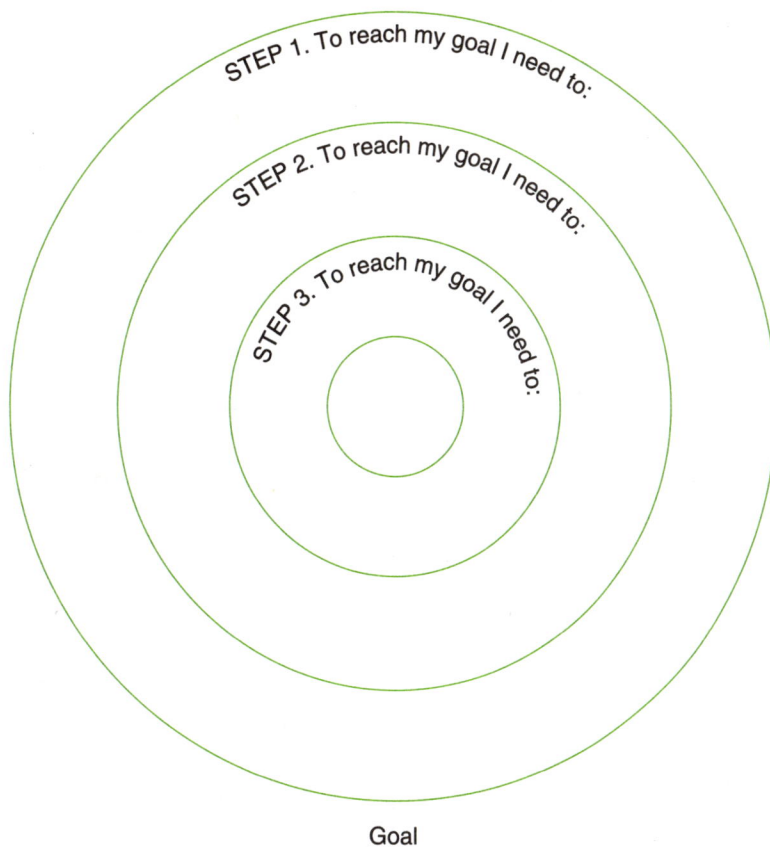

Goal

Personal Reflection:

Create a Bull's-Eye Book or blog. Students should create written reflections for each step toward the goal. Students can describe what actions were taken, challenges, and successes. Have them address whether or not their plan is working. Students should also address if they think their plan should be revised. Students may also rewrite or revise goals as needed. Ask: How does it feel to reach your goals?

Group Reflection:

- Why are goals important?
- What happens if you don't have any goals?
- What is the difference between long-term and short-term goals? Were your Bull's-Eye goals long or short term?
- What was it like to set your own goal?
- Is it okay to let others set goals for you? Why or why not?
- What areas of life could you have a goal in? School? Sports? Friends? Family?

Extended Learning:

Have students write interview questions about goal setting. Then ask them to interview and video record an adult about their long-term and short-term goals. Have students present their videos. Encourage them to add special effects to engage the audience.

Grades K-2: Spirit of Adventure Activities

Skills Within Reach

(20–30 MINUTES)

Common Core:
CCSS.ELA-LITERACY.SL.K-2.1
Participate in collaborative conversations with diverse partners about *grade K-2 topics and texts* with peers and adults in small and larger groups.

21st Century Skills:
Creativity and Innovation, Media Literacy

ISTE/NETS:
Creativity and innovation B

Spirit of Adventure:

Being excited to try new things, even if you don't know if you'll excel. Spirit of Adventure recognizes that as students set goals for themselves they need to understand their current skills and strengths.

Objective:

Students will be able to reflect on their current skills and strengths.

Materials:

Extra-large pieces of paper; markers.

Steps:

- Put students in groups of two.
- Give each student a sheet of paper large enough to trace around his or her body. Have students trace their partner's body on the paper while reaching or raising their hand.
- Inside the outline of the body, have students list all the academic or social skills they possess. Partners should help each other identify skills: speaking two languages, brushing my teeth, riding a bike, picking out my clothes, for example.
- Invite each group to share a few of these skills with their classmates.
- Next, have students identify skills they would like to learn. Ask students to write these skills on the outside of their traced bodies. Students can write these skills near their hand if they feel like they are close to developing this skill!
- Post the traced bodies around the room. Allow students to add skills to the inside and outside of the bodies for the next few weeks.

Personal Reflection:

Tell students it is important to celebrate all that we know and that we are always growing and learning new skills. Describe one new skill you would like to learn.

Group Reflection:

- What skills are you in reach of learning? How can you continue to work on these skills?
- Do you ever feel frustrated when you make mistakes or can't figure something out? How do you manage these feelings?

Extended Learning:

Remind students that skills can be improved by practice and playing. Allow students to play an education game to improve their skills. To improve math skills, play Math Ninja, Math and Letters Air Control, Rocket Math, MathBoard, Coin Catcher, or Mathemagics. Students who need help with their handwriting can use the iWriteWords app.

Notes:
___

Grades K-2: Spirit of Adventure Activities

Oh, the Places You'll Go

(40–50 MINUTES)

Common Core:

CCSS.ELA-LITERACY.RL.K.1
With prompting and support, ask and answer questions about key details in a text.

CCSS.ELA-LITERACY.RL.K.2
With prompting and support, retell familiar stories, including key details.

CCSS.ELA-LITERACY.RL.K.3
With prompting and support, identify characters, settings, and major events in a story.

CCSS.ELA-LITERACY.RL.1.1
Ask and answer questions about key details in a text.

CCSS.ELA-LITERACY.RL.1.2
Retell stories, including key details, and demonstrate understanding of their central message or lesson.

CCSS.ELA-LITERACY.RL.1.3
Describe characters, settings, and major events in a story, using key details.

CCSS.ELA-LITERACY.RL.2.1
Ask and answer such questions as *who, what, where, when, why*, and *how* to demonstrate understanding of key details in a text.

CCSS.ELA-LITERACY.RL.2.2
Recount stories, including fables and folktales from diverse cultures, and determine their central message, lesson, or moral.

Spirit of Adventure:

Being excited to try new things, even if you don't know if you'll excel.

Objective:

Students will be able to express where they would like to go.

Materials:

Oh, the Places You'll Go! by Dr. Seuss; hot air balloon template; string or ribbon, scissors, glue; picture of each student; Google earth app or Google maps.

Steps:

- Read *Oh, the Places You'll Go!* or play a YouTube recording of the story.
- Ask students to demonstrate their understanding of the story by retelling it as a class.
- Ask: What traits did the boy in the story have to help him continue to have a Spirit of Adventure when the journey was difficult? When have you had a Spirit of Adventure?
- As a class, discuss places students have been traveling and different journeys they have been on throughout their lives. Allow students to share experiences.
- Make a list of places students would like to go. As a class, use Google Earth to fly to different places or Google Maps and images to show pictures of different places. Allow students to research "places they would like to go." Allow students to think of dreams they would like to achieve as well.
- Pass out the hot air balloon and basket template. Students can write a sentence: I would like to go to _____ because _____. Or, I am on my way to _____.

- Next, ask students to tape or glue their picture in the basket. Cut out the template. Use string or ribbon to attach balloon and basket templates.
- Post hot air balloons throughout the room or on bulletin board.

Personal Reflection:

Will you need a Spirit of Adventure to get to the place on your hot air balloon? Explain.

Group Reflection:

- Do you need a Spirit of Adventure in school and in life?
- How is learning a journey?
- What places will we go as a class?

> **CCSS.ELA-LITERACY.RL.2.3**
> Describe how characters in a story respond to major events and challenges.
>
> **21st Century Skills:**
> Media, ICT Literacy, Creativity and Innovation, Social and Cross-Cultural Interaction
>
> **ISTE/NETS:**
> Creativity and innovation A, B, C
> Technology operations and concepts A, B
> Digital citizenship B, C, D

Extended Learning:

Students should create a road signpost with arrows facing in different directions to show all the different paths they can take! Give each student a craft stick. Provide students with foam arrows or construction paper. On each arrow, have students identify a job or path they would be interested in pursuing: dolphin trainer, learning to snorkel, science fair champion. Glue the arrows on the post.

Explore geography. Go to geoguessr.com and click let's play. Allow students to test their knowledge of geography. Students can see a picture and click on Google Maps guessing where the picture is from. The game will award points based on how close your guess is.

Have students search google maps for places they would like to go. Use Google Maps to create a collaborative map of places students will go! Check out other ideas at http://maps.google.com/help/maps/education/learn/index.html#development.

Notes:
_____
_____
_____
_____

Grades K-2: Spirit of Adventure Activities

Hands-On Goals

(20–30 MINUTES)

Common Core:
CCSS.ELA-LITERACY.W.1.2
Write informative/explanatory texts in which they name a topic, supply some facts about the topic, and provide some sense of closure.

CCSS.ELA-LITERACY.W.1.8
With guidance and support from adults, recall information from experiences or gather information from provided sources to answer a question.

21st Century Skills:
Initiative and Self-Direction, Productivity and Accountability, Collaboration, Creativity and Innovation

ISTE/NETS:
Communication and collaboration
Creativity and innovation A, B
Digital citizenship B, C, D

Spirit of Adventure:

Being excited to try new things, even if you don't know if you'll excel. Spirit of Adventure is about setting positive goals with students, not for students. This activity introduces students to goal setting in a fun and engaging way.

Objective:

Students will be able to identify a goal and corresponding action steps to achieve that goal.

Materials:

Construction paper, markers, scissors.

Steps:

- Warm-up discussion: What does it mean to set a goal for yourself? Why is it important to set goals?
- Begin by asking your students to think about something they would like to do better in school. What is something you want to learn this year? How do you think you could accomplish this goal?
- Let students know they are going to set a goal for themselves. As a class, brainstorm what some of these goals might be. Remember the goals should be obtainable, measurable, and simple.
- After each student has decided on a goal, give each student a piece of construction paper.
- Ask students to help each other trace one of their hands on the construction paper.
- Cut out the construction paper hands.
- Students should write their goal on the palm of the hand. On each of their fingers, have students write what they need to do to achieve their goal.
- Post the hands around the room.
- Every few days make sure students revisit their goals.

- Celebrate as students accomplish their goals and help others revise and rewrite their goals if necessary.
- Students will use their hands to celebrate success! Students should applaud and clap! Have students high five each other for accomplishing their goals.

Personal Reflection:

- Do all goals require action steps?
- What step was difficult for you? Did you achieve your goal?
- How did you feel when you achieved your goal?

Group Reflection:

Think about a challenge all students could participate in achieving. For example, maybe everyone will try to read two books a week for a month. Develop a way for everyone to keep track of the class challenge and celebrate at the end.

Extended Learning:

Show the *One Step at a Time Goal Achieving Cartoon Doodle* available at https://www.youtube.com/watch?v=8cCiqbSJ9fg. Using the ShowMe app, students will draw a picture of themselves on their way to achieving their goals. Students will record their voice to provide a narrative to the picture!

Notes:

_____
_____
_____
_____
_____
_____
_____

CHAPTER 7

Leadership & Responsibility

For several years students had complained to the librarian about the books that were available in the library. Through Facebook and other social media, students learned about good books, in many cases before the librarian knew they were available. Tightening budgets and the challenge of any one person keeping up with the plethora of middle school books published every year (many of them good) left students disappointed and the librarian frustrated. She raised this concern with the principal who suggested she put students on the library committee (made up of the librarian, a few ELA teachers, and a parent). Students are now brought into discussions about the budget (which help them apply what they are learning in math), about the need to buy enough books for the school's reading program, and about how to decide if a damaged book can be repaired or must be replaced. In addition, they bring their knowledge of what books students their age might like to read to the conversation. Helping the school solve these real-world problems took this group of students from passive grumblers to responsible school leaders.

One common way to think about leadership is in terms of roles. In this sense, student leadership is about student councils and team captains, the presidents of school clubs, and those chosen to lead the line to lunch. These positions are important and can teach young people important lessons in project management, organization, team building, and working with other students and adults. The downside of this view is that opportunities to be a leader in this way are limited. Typically, already organized, popular, confident, communicative students are chosen for these roles by their peers or teachers.

There is another way to think about leadership. In this other sense, everyone is called upon to *lead* his or her life. The opposite of leadership in the first sense is following; the opposite of leadership in this second sense is drifting. Each student we work with must learn the skills necessary to be an effective decision maker and then be given repeated opportunities to exercise those skills. Students must be given choices if they are going to learn leadership. Like any skill that develops over time, they will not always be successful. Students will make good choices and they will make poor choices. That is why leadership is partnered with responsibility.

In order to learn from both good and poor choices, students must be accountable for the decisions they make. Adults do young people a disservice when they clean up after them, when they assume responsibility for a student's misdeed, or when they otherwise short circuit the self-correcting process that is learning from one's mistakes. The natural consequence of not doing homework is not detention, but a failure to learn. The price to be paid for fighting with another student is not suspension, but a requirement to repair and restore the damage done to the relationship. Arbitrary consequences (in some schools arbitrarily applied) may maintain a semblance of order but do little to teach the important lessons associated with living a successful life.

The following exercises make clear the connection between options and outcomes. They will help your students think through their actions to the consequences of those actions. When young people learn that the decisions they make ultimately make them, they develop a sense of purpose and direction that will serve them well beyond school.

Grades 6-8: Leadership & Responsibility Activities

Tag Team Debate

(ABOUT 40 MINUTES)

Common Core:
CCSS.ELA-LITERACY.SL.6-8.1
Engage effectively in a range of collaborative discussions (one-on-one, in groups, and teacher-led) with diverse partners on grade 6-8 topics, texts, and issues, building on others' ideas and expressing their own clearly.

CCSS.ELA-LITERACY.SL.6-8.4
Present claims and findings, sequencing ideas logically and using pertinent descriptions, facts, and details to accentuate main ideas or themes; use appropriate eye contact, adequate volume, and clear pronunciation.

21st Century Skills:
Critical Thinking and Problem Solving, Communication, Collaboration

ISTE/NETS:
Critical thinking, problem solving and decision making D

Research and information fluency B, C

Communication and collaboration B, D

Leadership & Responsibility:

Leadership & Responsibility is about students feeling confident voicing their opinions and ideas. This activity encourages students to articulate opinions and listen respectfully to the opinions of others.

Objective:

Students will be able to articulate and voice their opinions while listening respectfully to the opinions of others.

Materials:

Devices with Popplet app for extended learning; six chairs.

Steps:

- What does it feel like to voice and defend an opinion? What is your overall opinion about school?
- Students should write down three controversial school issues that matter to students. This might include the dress code, homework policy, and discipline rules.
- Have the class resolve each of the issues into a statement. For example, "There should be a more relaxed dress code." "There should be no homework."
- Select one of the statements and randomly assign teams of five or six to make arguments either in favor of the statement (pro) or against it (con). Assign a third group as observers. Students need not actually agree with the position they are defending.
- Give students five to ten minutes to develop sound points in defense of the opinion their group must support. Have the observers anticipate the arguments others will make.

- Allow the pro and con groups to debate the issue by each putting forward three students to start the debate. Set up three chairs facing another three chairs. Other students on the team can have a seat at the debate table by tapping one of their classmates on the shoulder and taking their place. Only three students from each team can be debating at one time.
- After each debate, ask observers which side was more effective and why.
- Repeat with other topics. Rotate the groups so observers have a chance to debate.
- Make sure everyone gets a turn participating.

Personal Reflection:

- What was it like to argue for a position you do not agree with? What was it like to argue a position you do agree with?
- What did you learn from being an observer?
- Why do leaders need to consider both sides of an argument? Describe a situation when you considered both sides before making a decision.

Group Reflection:

What was difficult? What suggestions were most appealing? What would have helped the **debate** be stronger? Did anyone's viewpoint change? Why? Why not?

Extended Learning:

Invite students to research a controversial issue that you are interested in. Obtain evidence for **both** sides. Next, students should create a Popplet graphic organizer to display both sides of **the argument**.

Notes:
_____
_____
_____
_____
_____
_____

Grades 6-8: Leadership & Responsibility Activities

Drawing Dictations

(ABOUT 40 MINUTES)

Common Core:
CCSS.ELA-LITERACY.SL.6-8.4
Present claims and findings, sequencing ideas logically and using pertinent descriptions, facts, and details to accentuate main ideas or themes; use appropriate eye contact, adequate volume, and clear pronunciation.

CCSS.ELA-LITERACY.W.6-8.3
Write narratives to develop real or imagined experiences or events using effective technique, relevant descriptive details, and well-structured event sequences.

21st Century Skills:
Communication, Media Literacy, Leadership and Responsibility

ISTE/NETS:
Communication and collaboration

Technology operations and concepts D

Leadership & Responsibility:
Student leaders effectively speak and listen.

Objective:
Students will be able to create a replica of a diagram with a partner by using effective oral communication skills. Students will be able to discuss effective speaking and listening.

Materials:
Note cards, markers.

Steps:

- Pass out note cards and markers to each student. Ask students to create a diagram with various shapes, lines, letters, and numbers.
- Collect and shuffle cards.
- Next, have students form pairs and sit back to back. Determine Partner A and Partner B.
- Partner A will have a blank paper and markers. Partner B will have a diagram. Partner B should describe the diagram to his or her partner who will try to draw what he or she hears. Partner A cannot talk or ask questions.
- Partners then need to compare diagrams and get ready to switch roles. For the second round tell students the person drawing can now talk. Encourage partners to come up with a strategy for getting an accurate drawing. For example, students can decide they will ask each other questions and be more specific.
- Next, hand out a second diagram and have pairs repeat the exercise. Invite pairs to share pictures.
- Allow partners to show their diagrams. Have the whole group discuss their strategies and what helped with their communication.

Personal Reflection:

- Write about a time when you had to use effective speaking skills.
- Write about a time when you had to use effective listening skills.

Group Reflection:

Source: Photo by Julie Hellerstein.

- What helped improve communication from the first to second round? What did each person do differently?
- As leaders in a school community, what can we do to help make sure we are being understood when we speak? What can we do to make sure we understand when we listen?
- What kind of a communicator should a student leader be? Can a student be a quiet, introverted leader? Explain.
- What makes a leader an effective communicator?
- Why do you think some students don't voice their opinions and ideas?

Extended Learning:

Students can practice their communication skills by using the ShowMe app and draw or describe a picture. Using the ShowMe app, students can draw a caricature of an effective leader and describe his or her characteristics and communication skills.

Notes:

Grades 6-8: Leadership & Responsibility Activities

Values Auction

(ABOUT 40 MINUTES)

Common Core:
CCSS.ELA-LITERACY.SL.6-8.1
Engage effectively in a range of collaborative discussions (one-on-one, in groups, and teacher-led) with diverse partners on grade 6-8 topics, texts, and issues, building on others' ideas and expressing their own clearly.

CCSS.ELA-LITERACY.W.6-8.1
Write arguments to support claims with clear reasons and relevant evidence.

21st Century Skills:
Communication, Collaboration, Leadership and Responsibility

ISTE/NETS:
Communication and collaboration D

Critical thinking, problem solving, and decision making C, D

Leadership & Responsibility:

Student leaders often need to clarify what values are most important.

Objective:

Students will be able to evaluate what values are important by collaborating and discussing with peers.

Materials:

Fourteen flash cards with the following words written on them: *Charity, Peace, Honesty, Wisdom, Health, Artistic Talent, Athleticism, Love, Patience, Happiness, Family, Wealth, Beauty, Trust*; play money for four or five teams (we recommend playing with five $500 and ten $1,000 in paper money—a total of $12,500).

Steps:

- Ask students what they know about an auction. Explain that at an auction people bid against each other for items they really want.
- Ask: What values are important to you? Explain that in this activity, students will be bidding for the values they want in their lives.
- Post the value cards on the board: *Charity, Peace, Honesty, Wisdom, Health, Artistic Talent, Athleticism, Love, Patience, Happiness, Family, Wealth, Beauty,* and *Trust*.
- Students should work with teams to bid for the values they want and think are most important.
- Conduct the auction. Allow students to bid and hand cards to highest bidder.
- Students are able to buy more than one value but may not overspend.

Source: Photo by Julie Hellerstein.

Personal Reflection:

Describe a situation when you had to clarify your values. How do you resolve conflicts between what is valuable and what is satisfying?

Group Reflection:

- Which values were most highly contested? Why?
- Which were not? Why?
- What does society value most? Provide a rationale.
- What do we value at school most?
- As a leader, why is it important to clarify your values?

Extended Learning:

Option 1: Students should work in small groups to reach a decision about the following fictitious dilemma. Using Edmodo or an online forum, the group should explain their decision and how they reached their decision. Students should comment and discuss.

The ship is sinking and the seas are rough. All but one lifeboat has been destroyed. The lifeboat holds a maximum of six people. There are ten people who want to board the lifeboat. The four individuals who do not board the boat will certainly die. Argue for who should stay.

- Woman who thinks she is six-weeks pregnant
- Lifeguard
- Two young adults who recently married
- Senior citizen who has fifteen grandchildren
- Elementary school teacher
- Thirteen-year-old twins
- Veteran nurse
- Captain of the ship

Option 2: Students should comment and discuss school scenarios:

Social Media Student Suspension: A student is getting a ten-day suspension for creating a fake Twitter account that posts mean remarks about teachers and students. The principal doesn't seem to like this student and he usually gets in trouble. You know that it was actually someone else who did it, someone who never gets in trouble, and that the principal seems to like. What do you do?

Cheater Cross Country: You run cross-country for your school. During a race, one of your teammates whispers to you that she knows a short cut and you won't get caught. Around the next turn in the trail, she takes a hard left and no one sees her take the short cut. Your team wins the meet. What do you do?

Gossip Girls and Guys: Your friends are talking badly about someone. They are saying things that you know are not true but are really scandalous. They ask your opinion. How do you handle this situation?

Detention: During class you threw something across the room. The teacher blames someone else and gives him a detention. If you get another detention, you will get suspended and won't be able to play in your sport this weekend. What do you do?

What Is Fair?: The principal asks you to help organize an assembly for students. You can choose five students to help you with this project. Many students want to help. How do you choose students in a way that is fair?

The iPad: You take your tests on an iPad. You can easily access your notes during the test, but the teacher doesn't know. A lot of students are doing this. What do you do and why?

The Change in the Cafeteria: After paying for lunch, you realize the cafeteria worker gave you too much change. What should you consider in making your decision? What will happen to the cafeteria worker?

Grades 3-5: Leadership & Responsibility Activities

My Voice and Choice

(ABOUT 30 MINUTES)

Leadership & Responsibility:

Leadership & Responsibility is about students feeling confident in expressing their opinions and ideas. This activity encourages students to think about voice and their opinions.

Objective:

Students will be able to defend their opinion or preference through writing. Students will be able to evaluate whether they have a voice at school.

Materials:

You will need to create a list of pairs prior to the activity; tape; a survey tool for extended learning.

> **Common Core:**
> CCSS.ELA-LITERACY.W.3-5.1
> Write opinion pieces on topics or texts, supporting a point of view with reasons.
>
> **21st Century Skills:**
> Critical Thinking and Problem Solving, Leadership and Responsibility, Initiative and Self-Direction
>
> **ISTE/NETS:**
> Critical thinking, problem solving, and decision making A, B
> Technology operations and concepts A
> Digital citizenship D

Steps:

- Prior to the activity, create twelve pairs of words. Examples can be chocolate or vanilla, two rival sports teams, winter or summer, beach or mountains, juice or milk, math or reading, indoor recess or outdoor recess, packing your lunch or cafeteria food, waking up early or staying up late, video games or playing outside, reading silently or reading aloud.

- Use the following writing prompt: What does it mean to voice your opinion? What is your opinion about school?

- Discuss with the class the importance of making choices that are meaningful to them. Ask: What decisions do you wish you had a choice in that you currently do not?

- Have all the students gather in the middle of the room. Mark off a line between the front of the room and the back of the room. You may use tape or another visible marking. Explain to students that they will be making a choice and for each pair of words they should move and stand by their preference. For example, "I will call out chocolate (point to front of room) or vanilla (point to back of room) and you will physically walk and go stand at the line to show which you prefer."

- For each pair of words, remember to point where to go for each option.

- After students choose their sides, regroup in the middle of the room, and allow some students to give reasons why they chose what they did. Generate conversation.
- Repeat this exercise until all the pairs of words are used.
- Discuss with your students how they made their choices and what influenced them.

Personal Reflection:

Select one of the choices that you made. Write a persuasive paragraph justifying your choice. Next, describe a time when you had a choice or voice in school.

Group Reflection:

- What influenced your choices in this activity? Did your peers influence you? Did you follow your friends?
- How did you express your opinions and voice in this activity? How do leaders share their ideas with others? How do leaders get the opinions of others?
- Leaders have their own opinions and do not always agree with the opinions of others. Did this happen during the activity? Does this happen in school? Has this happened in politics or current events?

Extended Learning:

Have a discussion about students having a voice at school. Ask: Do you think students at school are able to share what they think about school and their experiences being a student at your school?

As a class, invent a student voice feedback system that will allow students to share their opinions about school using a technology tool of their choice. Research options can be Socrative, TodaysMeet.com, Edmodo, or Survey Monkey. What kinds of questions should be asked? As a class or in small groups, have students generate questions. How will we make sure students feel comfortable with using their voice? Who could use this tool? When? With permission from key players, pilot your student voice feedback system.

Notes:
_____
_____
_____
_____
_____

Grades 3-5: Leadership & Responsibility Activities

Addressing Assumptions

(ABOUT 40 MINUTES)

Leadership & Responsibility:

Leadership & Responsibility encourages all students to develop leadership skills. Students often make assumptions without knowing all the facts. This activity introduces students to the notion that our assumptions are not always correct.

Objective:

Students will be able to apply the concept that assumptions are not always correct.

Materials:

Device with Socrative teacher app; devices for students with Socrative student app. Socrative is a clicker response system.

Steps:

- Before the lesson: Download the teacher Socrative app and set up an account. You will set up a room number that you will give your students to enter the room. Make it easy for them to remember, perhaps your last name and actual room number.
    - Next, click Manage Quizzes: Create, Edit, and Import Quizzes.
    - Click Import Quiz>Import Shared Quiz. Then type in, SOC-4188223.
    - Go back to the main screen and then select start Quiz.
    - Then select the quiz you imported (copy of Addressing Assumptions).
    - Then select student-paced quiz.
- Students should use the Socrative Student app. They can join the room by entering the room number. The quiz will automatically start. Students should enter their name for the first question. Next they will finish writing the statements.
    - Question 1 of 9: He laughed loudly because . . .
    - Question 2 of 9: She ran away because . . .

Common Core:
CCSS.ELA-LITERACY.W.3-5.4
Produce clear and coherent writing in which the development and organization are appropriate to task, purpose, and audience

CCSS.ELA-LITERACY.W.3-5.10
Write routinely over extended time frames (time for research, reflection, and revision) and shorter time frames (a single sitting or a day or two) for a range of discipline-specific tasks, purposes, and audiences.

21st Century Skills:
ICT Literacy, Critical Thinking and Problem Solving

ISTE/NETS:
Technology operations and concepts A, B, C, D
Critical thinking, problem solving, and decision making D

CHAPTER 7: LEADERSHIP & RESPONSIBILITY

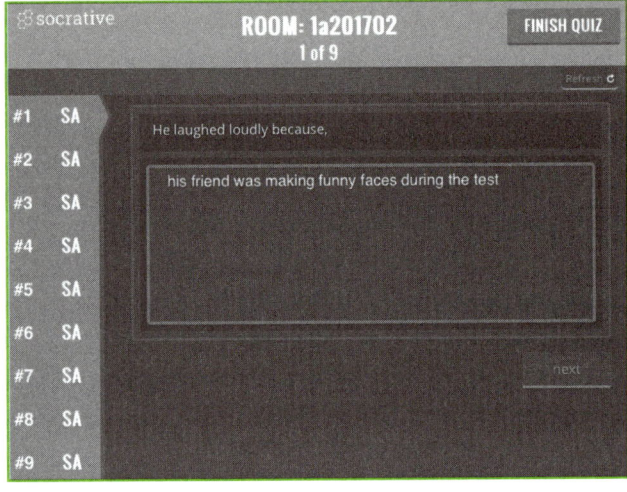

Source: Created using Socrative.

- Question 3 of 9: She was sad because . . .
- Question 4 of 9: He did not finish his homework because . . .
- Question 5 of 9: She ran so hard because . . .
- Question 6 of 9: The teacher was upset at his class because . . .
- Question 7 of 9: She was late to school because . . .
- Question 8 of 9: Her friends like her because . . .
- Question 9 of 9: He is good at math because . . .

- Next, students should click Finish Quick Quiz or if students are sharing a device click Let another student take the quiz.
- You may see the live results on your app, when students are finished. Click End Quiz and have a report e-mailed to you.
- The report contains all of the students' responses to the questions.
- Project the report on the board and have students share and read different responses.
- Ask students to think about all the different responses and assumptions that their classmates made during this exercise.

Personal Reflection:

- Describe a situation when you or someone you know failed to gather all the facts before you made an assumption. What was the outcome?
- Describe a situation when you gathered facts before making an assumption. What was the outcome?

Group Reflection:

In small groups, students will share their personal reflections: When have you made an assumption before you had all the facts? When have you waited to get all the facts? Why do we make assumptions about each other?

Explain and discuss the following points:

- Leaders spend time gathering all the facts and not jumping to conclusions.
- When we communicate with others, people may hear something different from what we mean.
- Responsible leaders explain why they make their decision and how their decisions will affect others.

Extended Learning:

Lead a discussion: How can assumptions lead to stereotypes and unfair judgments about individuals and groups?

Check out lesson plans about Learning to Respect Each Other from Discovery Education at http://www.discoveryeducation.com/teachers/free-lesson-plans/learning-to-respect-each-other.cfm.

Create an Addressing Assumptions Board. When students have an assumption, they can write down the assumption. Next, they should spend time researching that assumption. Once they have researched, they should post on the board. This is one way we can learn from each other. Students can also use the board to write down misconceptions and assumptions in history, science, math, and how they got corrected. Ask: How do you make inferences?

Notes:

Grades 3-5: Leadership & Responsibility Activities

Discuss and Decide

(ABOUT 30 MINUTES)

Common Core:
CCSS.ELA-LITERACY.SL.3-5.1
Engage effectively in a range of collaborative discussions (one-on-one, in groups, and teacher-led) with diverse partners on *grade 3-5 topics and texts*, building on others' ideas and expressing their own clearly.

21st Century Skills:
Leadership and Responsibility, Critical Thinking and Problem Solving

ISTE/NETS:
Research and information fluency B
Critical thinking, problem solving and decision making D

Leadership & Responsibility:
Leadership & Responsibility is about students making decisions. All too often students wait to see what decisions other people make and then just agree. This activity asks students to think about some situations and decide what they might do in each.

Objective:
Students will be able to identify leadership behavior in various situations.

Materials:
Decision making cards.

Steps:
- Warm-up discussion: What types of decisions do you make every day? How do you make a decision?
- Break students into groups of three.
- Give each group a few scenario cards. After the groups have finished discussing, bring the class together.
    - **Gossip:** While out at recess, you overhear some students talking about another student. You cannot believe what they are saying. Is it true? You want to say something, but then the group might talk about you. What do you do?
    - **She Took My Homework:** While at lunch, you and some other students were working on your homework. In class when you go to turn in your papers, you notice that someone has yours. The other student claims it is hers. What do you do?
    - **Last Pick:** In gym class, your teacher asks you to be a captain and choose students for the team. You are excited to be the captain. When it comes time to pick teammates, you immediately pick the best players. Then you notice the kids who are still waiting to be picked. They look nervous and sad. What do you do?

- **Homework Help:** You have a big assignment due for school. Your sister says she remembers doing the same assignment and she might even have her old copy. You could just use her assignment and make everything easy. What would you do?
- **Extra Money:** Your class is collecting money for a field trip. One student is in charge of all the money. He thinks you have already paid and you know you never paid. Your mom gave you money this morning, but you could really use the extra money for something else. What do you do?
- **Teasing:** Walking to class, you hear older kids making fun of a student who dresses differently. The kid walks away, but you know it bothers her. You can keep walking or say something, but then you might be teased. What do you do?
- **Project People:** Your teacher puts you in a group with three students you do not like. As a group you must work together for two days. The other students talk all the time and don't seem to listen to you or your ideas. What do you do?
- **My Voice and Choice:** Your teacher has asked you for one suggestion to make the class a better place for all students. You can think of many ideas that would make the class better for you personally. What suggestion do you make to your teacher?
- **Substitute Shenanigans:** Some of your friends want to play a trick on the substitute teacher. You do not think anyone will get hurt and you think it's funny. What do you do?

- Talk with the class about how they made decisions. Ask: What was difficult about making their decisions, and what they decided in each situation?

Personal Reflection:

Pick one of the following individual challenges. Reflect on what you learned.

- Admit your mistakes next time you are wrong.
- Share your opinions and ideas about your classroom with your teacher.
- Make your own decisions rather than following your friends.
- Write a letter to the principal suggesting an idea to improve the school.
- Read an editorial in a local paper. Write back to the paper in response.

Group Reflection:

Talk through each scenario and identify positive and negative consequences. Do good leaders think about the positive and negative consequences beforehand? When have you thought about the consequences before making a decision? List examples on the board.

Sometimes there is not a right and a wrong decision; rather, we have to choose between two rights. Have students generate examples.

Gossip: While out at recess, you overhear some students talking about another student. You cannot believe what they are saying. Is it true? You want to say something, but then the group might talk about you. What do you do?	**She Took My Homework:** While at lunch, you and some other students were working on your homework. In class when you go to turn in your papers, you notice that someone has yours. The other student claims it is hers. What do you do?	**Last Pick:** In gym class, your teacher asks you to be a captain and choose students for the team. You are excited to be the captain. When it comes time to pick teammates you immediately pick the best players. Then you notice the kids who are still waiting to be picked. They look nervous and sad. What do you do?
Homework Help: You have a big assignment due for school. Your sister says she remembers doing the same assignment and she might even have her old copy. You could just use her assignment and make everything easy. What would you do?	**Extra Money:** Your class is collecting money for a field trip. One student is in charge of all the money. He thinks you have already paid and you know you never paid. Your mom gave you money this morning but you could really use the extra money for something else. What do you do?	**Teasing:** Walking to class, you hear older kids making fun of a student who dresses differently. The kid walks away, but you know it bothers her. You can keep walking or say something, but then you might be teased. What do you do?
Project People: Your teacher puts you in a group with three students you do not like. As a group you must work together for two days. The other students talk all the time and don't seem to listen to you or your ideas. What do you do?	**My Voice and Choice:** Your teacher has asked you for one suggestion to make the class a better place for all students. You can think of many ideas that would make the class better for you personally. What suggestion do you make to your teacher?	**Substitute Shenanigans:** Some of your friends want to play a trick on the substitute teacher. You do not think anyone will get hurt and you think it's funny. What do you do?

Extended Learning:

People of all ages can be leaders. As a class, create a collaborative Young Leader List. Each student should share a link to an article, video, commercial, or book passage about a young leader and describe their leadership traits.

One example is Alanna Wall, a twelve-year-old girl who loves art, nail design, and helping people. She started an organization called Polished Girlz (http://polishedgirlz.org/about-alanna/). Here is a video clip of her on *The Ellen DeGeneres Show*: https://www.youtube.com/watch?v=KH7y_EQM2Sk.

Notes:
_____
_____
_____
_____
_____
_____
_____
_____
_____
_____
_____
_____
_____
_____
_____

Grades K-2: Leadership & Responsibility Activities

Listening Blocks

(ABOUT 30 MINUTES)

Common Core:
CCSS.ELA-LITERACY.SL.K-2.1 Participate in collaborative conversations with diverse partners about *grade K-2 topics and texts* with peers and adults in small and larger groups.

CCSS.ELA-LITERACY.SL.2.5 Create audio recordings of stories or poems; add drawings or other visual displays to stories or recounts of experiences when appropriate to clarify ideas, thoughts, and feelings.

21st Century Skills:
Communication, Media Literacy, Leadership and Responsibility

ISTE/NETS:
Communication and collaboration D
Technology operations and concepts D

Leadership & Responsibility:

Leadership & Responsibility encourages all students to develop leadership skills. Listening to others is one key component of being a good leader.

Objective:

Students will be able to communicate and listen to each other to build a structure.

Materials:

Building blocks; devices with Pic Stitch (optional).

Steps:

- Warm-up discussion: What does it mean to be a good listener? Why is it difficult to be a good listener? How can we be better listeners?
- Put students into groups of two.
- Give each group a handful of building blocks.
- Let students know they are going to practice listening to each other.
- Students should sit back to back.
- Student A should build a simple structure using building blocks without letting Student B see the structure.
- Next, Student A should try to get Student B to build the same structure without looking at each other. Student B cannot ask questions and must just listen and build.
- After students have completed their structures, have them see how similar their structures are. If students are working with devices, have students make a picture collage of the two structures using PicStitch.
- Discuss how to make communication and listening more effective and then have the partners switch roles. Allow students to ask questions this time. Explain the importance of giving clear directions with detailed information.

Source: © Ingram Publishing/Thinkstock Photos

Personal Reflection:

- Ask students to give themselves a score of 1 to 10 on how well they gave directions. Next, ask students to give themselves a score on how they listened.

- Have students write a story or draw a picture about a time when it was important to be a good listener.

Group Reflection:

- Have groups share their strategies. Highlight groups that listened to each other well. Why is it important for leaders to be good listeners? Why is it important for leaders to listen to others' ideas? Name a leader who listens to others' ideas.

- Next, play a quick game of telephone. Students will whisper a sentence into each other's ears and the last student will say it aloud. Compare the original sentence and the new sentence. Discuss: When we communicate with other people, they often hear something different than we meant. Did this happen in telephone? When did this happen in the building block activity?

- Do leaders ever make mistakes and try again? Did this happen to you during the building block activity? Why do leaders need to keep trying after they make mistakes? Give examples of when it took you many times before you got something right.

Extended Learning:

Have students create a list of what NOT listening looks like. Give examples of when someone was not listening to you. Have students act out ways to show you are not listening. Next, students can create a public service announcement about effective listening.

Have students research how to be a good communicator. For example, good listeners use eye contact, ask questions to find out more, repeat what they heard in their own words. Next, students can use the ShowMe or Educreations app to draw a picture of a good communicator while recording a description of a good communicator.

Notes:

_____

_____

Grades K-2: Leadership & Responsibility Activities

What Do You Think?

(ABOUT 30 MINUTES)

Common Core:
CCSS.ELA-LITERACY.SL.2.4
Tell a story or recount an experience with appropriate facts and relevant, descriptive details, speaking audibly in coherent sentences.

CCSS.ELA-LITERACY.SL.K-2.1
Participate in collaborative conversations with diverse partners about *grade K-2 topics and texts* with peers and adults in small and larger groups.

CCSS.MATH.CONTENT.2.MD.C.8
Solve word problems involving dollar bills, quarters, dimes, nickels, and pennies, using $ and ¢ symbols appropriately.

21st Century Skills:
Leadership and Responsibility, Initiative and Self-Direction, Critical Thinking and Problem Solving

ISTE/NETS:
Critical thinking, problem solving, and decision making C, D

Research and information fluency B, C, D

Leadership & Responsibility:

Leadership & Responsibility is about students making decisions. All too often students wait to see the decisions other people make and then just agree. This activity asks students to think about specific situations and then think about what they might do in each situation.

Objective:

Students will be able to identify what actions a student leader would take in difficult situations.

Materials:

What do you think? list.

Steps:

- Give each group of students the *What do you think?* list.
- Put students in groups of three.
- Let students know they are going to be talking about situations on the list in their groups.
- Read the first scenario. Ask each individual to think about what they would do. Prompt students to draw from their experience.
- Next, have the group discuss that scenario with their small group. Then, discuss with the larger group.
- Scaffold students to think and talk about the other scenarios on the page. Use think-pair-share.

What Do You Think?

Whose Turn Is It?

You and your friends are playing on the playground. The game requires you to take turns. Your friend thinks it is his turn, but you are sure it is your turn. You begin to argue. How do you decide what to do?

You're Out!

During gym class you are playing baseball. Your opponent slides into home plate and you tag him out. The other team says their player is safe. An argument follows. How do you decide if the player is out or safe?

Project Time!

Your teacher has put you in a group with two students you don't really like. As a group, you must work together for two days. The other students don't really talk much or give ideas. What do you do?

My Favorite Flick

Your siblings are watching your favorite movie. You have a big project to work on that you need to do well on. You don't have enough time to watch the movie and work on the project. What do you do?

Oops!

After your class went to lunch, you accidentally broke your teacher's favorite mug. No one saw you break the mug and you know your teacher is going to be upset. What do you do?

Embarrassing Picture Post

One of your friends has taken an embarrassing picture of a classmate and is spreading it around school. What do you do?

Bathroom Stall Bully

Someone wrote something mean about the teacher in the bathroom stall. If your teacher reads it, you are scared she will be upset. You think one of the cool kids wrote it and you do not want someone to write something mean about you. What do you do?

My Voice and Choice

Your teacher has asked you for one suggestion to make the class a better place for all students. You would like to move your desk to make the class better for you. This really does not help other students. What suggestion would you make to your teacher?

Cheating

After a spelling test, your teacher calls you and your friend to the desk. The teacher wonders why both of you missed the same word. You think your friend cheated off your paper and she says you cheated off her paper. What do you do?

Personal Reflection:

Before making a decision, it is important to think about the positive and negative consequences of your decision. Write or tell about an experience where you had to make a big decision. What did you consider? What was the outcome?

Group Reflection:

- What situation was the toughest? Why?
- How did you reach your decision? What did you think about?
- Leaders seek advice and opinions of others before making many decisions. When have you gotten advice and other opinions before making a decision?
- Can you learn from adults? Can you learn from each other?
- What decisions do you make every day? How to use your free time? How to spend a gift card or allowance? What to wear?

Extended Learning:

Students can explore fiscal responsibility through playing, reading, and taking fun and interactive quizzes. Have students visit TheMint.org/kids. Some features include the article "7 Ways Kids Can Earn Money," the Be Your Own Boss Challenge, savings tricks, the Spending Quiz, and various scenarios about giving and helping out. Give students math word problems involving money as a follow-up.

Notes:

_____

_____

_____

_____

_____

_____

_____

_____

Grades K-2: Leadership & Responsibility Activities

Opportunity for Opinions

(ABOUT 30 MINUTES)

Leadership & Responsibility:

Leadership & Responsibility is about students feeling confident in voicing their opinions and ideas. This activity encourages students to think about and voice their opinions.

Objective:

Students will be able to voice their opinions and provide reasoning for their opinions.

Materials:

You will need to create a list of pairs prior to this activity.

Steps:

- Warm-up discussion: What does it mean to voice your opinion? What is your opinion about school?
- Formulate numerous either/or questions and statements.
    - Would you rather have a cat or dog for a pet?
    - Do you prefer lemon or lime?
    - I'm giving you a snack; do you want it to be chocolate or vanilla?
    - Which season is more fun: winter or summer?
    - Would you rather color with crayons or markers?
    - Do you prefer math or reading?
    - Would you rather sing or dance?
    - Would you rather play at indoor recess or outdoor recess?
- Discuss with the class the importance of expressing their opinion.

Common Core:
CCSS.ELA-LITERACY.W.K.1
Use a combination of drawing, dictating, and writing to compose opinion pieces in which they tell a reader the topic or the name of the book they are writing about and state an opinion or preference about the topic or book.

CCSS.ELA-LITERACY.W.1.1
Write opinion pieces in which they introduce the topic or name the book they are writing about, state an opinion, supply a reason for the opinion, and provide some sense of closure.

CCSS.ELA-LITERACY.W.2.1
Write opinion pieces in which they introduce the topic or book they are writing about, state an opinion, supply reasons that support the opinion, use linking words (e.g., *because*, *and*, *also*) to connect opinion and reasons, and provide a concluding statement or section.

21st Century Skills:
Critical Thinking and Problem Solving, Leadership and Responsibility, Initiative and Self-Direction

ISTE/NETS:
Critical thinking, problem solving, and decision making A, B

Digital literacy B

Technology operations and concepts A, B, C, D

- Have all the students line up in the middle of the room. Explain to students that they will be making a choice and for each pair of words, they can either stand and throw their hands in the air or squat to show their preference. If you like the first option, you will stand and throw your hands up, if you like the second option you will squat. For example, "I ask chocolate (stand) or vanilla (squat) and you will stand or squat to show your choice."
- For each pair of words, remember to specify stand or squat.
- After students strike their pose, allow some students to give reasons why they chose what they did. Generate conversation.
- Repeat this exercise until all the pairs of words are used.
- Discuss with your students how they made their choices and what influenced them.

Personal Reflection:

Select one of the choices you made in the activity. Example: Would you rather have a dog for a pet or a cat? Using a graphic organizer, write a topic sentence that states your opinion, three reasons, and a conclusion sentence. Allow students to research to come up with their reasons.

- My Opinion:
- Reason 1:
- Reason 2:
- Reason 3:
- Conclusion:

Find a picture online or draw a picture that supports your opinion.

Group Reflection:

- What influenced your choices in this activity? Did your peers influence you? Did you follow your friends?
- How did you express your opinions and voice in this activity? How do leaders share their ideas with others? How do leaders get the opinions of others?
- Leaders have their own opinions and do not always agree with the opinions of others. Did this happen during the activity? Does this happen in school? Has this happened in politics or current events?
- What opinions do you have about this class? What is your favorite part? What would you like to see change that would benefit all students?

Extended Learning:

Design a webquest or QR code scavenger hunt that sends students to ten different pictures. The pictures should be abstract or difficult to know the meaning of. Let students know that you want their opinions and ideas on what the pictures represent. Inform your students that you are not looking for the correct answers; rather, you want to know what they think. Sit in a circle and listen to each other's opinions. Discuss what it means to have an opinion and why it is important to voice your opinion.

CHAPTER 8

Confidence to Take Action

> Service learning develops purpose and confidence in students. Schools that see service learning not just as a hoop to jump through to get credit but recognize it as an opportunity to make a real difference in their community and the world instill in their students a sense of efficacy and citizenship. Beyond collecting food or clothing during holiday time, service learning provides regular experiences at local soup kitchens, visits to elder care facilities to read and discuss the newspaper with guests who have failing eyesight, and a regular presence at animal shelters to help care for animals that have been abused or abandoned. All of this is tied into a curriculum that helps students in age-appropriate ways write about and reflect on the myriad social, psychological, economic, political, and global causes and effects of what they are encountering.

Confidence to Take Action is a reciprocal phenomenon: I need confidence in order to act and I need to act in order to build confidence. There is a bit of chicken and egg involved. A lack of self-assurance can be paralyzing; a lack of action can create insecurity. Where to begin if as educators we want to nurture Confidence to Take Action on our students?

There must be the right relationship between a student's skill level on the one hand and a teacher's expectations and support of them on the other hand. When a teacher expects ever so slightly more of a student than she feels capable of and provides ever so slightly less support than a student feels she needs, the student strives to meet the expectations of the teacher while trusting that the teacher will provide help if needed. If expectations are too high above the student's skill level or the support too far below her skill level, she flounders and fails and confidence takes a blow. If the expectations are too low or the support too much, the student lives down to expectations or sees the teacher as a crutch—in either case confidence is not cultivated. But in the right bandwidth of support, skill, and expectation, Confidence to Take Action develops and grows.

The challenge, of course, is that as confidence grows and so ability, expectations must be adjusted ever higher even as support trails ever so slightly behind the improving skill. Anyone who has ever seen a parent teach a child to ride a bicycle has seen this interplay at work. The right balance is difficult to find. There will be tumbles and falls. But each time we help students brush off the dust and get back on—whether the bike or the pronunciation of a word or the integration of an equation—they mature in self-confidence and learn to act on behalf of their dreams and goals.

The activities in this chapter help produce a confidence that can be easily transferred to other parts of a young person's life. By developing a fundamental belief in one's abilities and competence as a person, students can take on other challenges at school, at home, in their work, and in life. By exercising confidence using these activities, students will build a belief in themselves that will help them be successful academically, personally, and socially.

Grades 6-8: Confidence to Take Action Activities

Time Capsule

(ABOUT 50 MINUTES)

Confidence to Take Action:
Confidence to Take Action is about thinking of your future and doing something to make that future happen.

Objective:
Students will be able to reflect on their confidence and accomplishments by creating a personal time capsule that they will revisit at the end of the school year.

Materials:
One container for each student: Containers should be the size of a small box (e.g., a small can, coffee can); time capsule sheet; decorating materials.

Steps:
- Warm-up discussion: What does it mean to be confident? What does it mean to be proud of who and what you are doing? What do you hope to accomplish by the end of the year?
- Have students create a *K-W-L* chart and research on time capsules. Find relevant articles to frame the activity. For example, have students read articles about the 1795 time capsule found in Boston (Samuel Adams and Paul Revere).
- Let students know that they are going to be putting together their own time capsule. Ask students what type of items might go in a time capsule and why.
- Give each student a time capsule container to decorate.
- Students should fill out the time capsule worksheet.
- Next, have students put at least five things in the time capsule: the time capsule worksheet, a piece of writing or artwork, and three things that represent them now. Students may need to bring these items from home so plan accordingly with due dates.
- Have students seal the time capsules and put them away until the end of the year.
- At the end of the year, open the time capsules and let students share their items as well as how they have grown over the course of the year.
- This activity can be done for short-term goals as well. Time capsules can be put away for a month or several months.

Common Core:
CCSS.ELA-LITERACY.W.6.10
Write routinely over extended time frames (time for research, reflection, and revision) and shorter time frames (a single sitting or a day or two) for a range of discipline-specific tasks, purposes, and audiences.

21st Century Skills:
Creativity and Innovation, Collaboration, Social and Cross-Cultural Interaction

ISTE/NETS:
Research and information fluency B
Creativity and innovation B, D
Communication and collaboration D
Digital citizenship A, B

Time Capsule Worksheet

1. What is today's date?

2. What is the weather like today?

3. What specifically are you wearing today?

4. What songs have you most recently listened to?

5. What just happened on your favorite TV show or book that you are currently reading?

6. What is your funniest or happiest recent memory?

7. Describe the person you are today.

8. What is your personal motto or philosophy?

9. List a few things you hope to learn over the course of the year.

10. How do you hope to grow personally by the end of the school year?

11. What do you hope your friends will say about you at the end of the year?

12. What do you think will be your biggest challenge this year?

13. Describe a recent accomplishment.

14. What are your life goals at the moment?

15. What will some of your successes be?

Copyright © 2015 by Corwin. All rights reserved. Reprinted from *Student Voice: Turn Up the Volume K–8 Activity Book* by Russell J. Quaglia, Michael J. Corso, and Julie Hellerstein. Thousand Oaks, CA: Corwin, www.corwin.com. Reproduction authorized only for the local school site or nonprofit organization that has purchased this book.

Personal Reflection:

- After making the time capsule: What was it like to visualize your goals and dreams? How important is it to think about your future?
- At the end of the year: What surprised you most about your time capsule? What have you accomplished since your time capsule? How have you changed? What has stayed the same?

Group Reflection:

Develop a time capsule that represents what it means to be a student at your school in the current year. Write letters to the future students and encourage students to be confident. Bury it and decide a date when it can be opened—for example, for a social studies class to open in the year 2045.

Extended Learning:

Students who are over 13 years old: Timehop is an app that gives you a daily feed of your old photos, Facebook, Twitter, Instagram, and camera roll photos. Have students create new material for their future selves to post today that will go into their Timehop the next year. Next, have students reflect on their past social media posts. Discuss digital citizenship. Have students write and reflect on past memories.

Students who are under 13 years old: Review pictures from the past on your device. Do you see any pictures where you had a lot of self-confidence? How could you tap into previous experiences of acting with confidence today? Discuss digital citizenship.

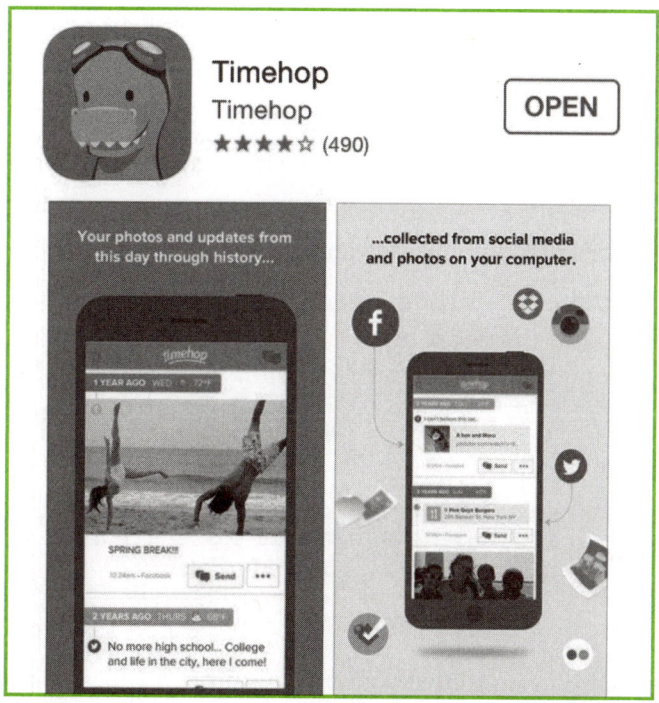

Source: Courtesy of Timehop.

CHAPTER 8: CONFIDENCE TO TAKE ACTION

Grades 6-8: Confidence to Take Action Activities

Extreme Community Makeover

(ABOUT 50 MINUTES)

Common Core:
CCSS.ELA-LITERACY.W.6-8.7
Conduct short research projects to answer a question, drawing on several sources and refocusing the inquiry when appropriate.

21st Century Skills:
Critical Thinking and Problem Solving, Creativity and Innovation, Collaboration

ISTE/NETS:
Research and information fluency A

Communication and collaboration A, D

Creativity and innovation A, B, C, D

Confidence to Take Action:
Confidence to Take Action is about making a difference in the school, community, and world. All students can dream about and act upon what differences they can make.

Objective:
Students will be able to create a plan of action for a cause they believe in.

Materials:
Materials may vary depending on student projects; most will need devices or computers with Internet access.

Steps:
- Put students in groups of three or four.
- Let students know they are going to have an opportunity to build a better community.
- Students should begin by brainstorming their ideal community. What would be different? Why?
- Allow students to research community transformation projects from other cities.
- After brainstorming, students will represent their new community through pictures, social media posts, Minecraft or a build-a-city video game or app, videos, stories, a collage or other display that represents their vision.
- Next, students will research or write a proposal of a small change they could take to work toward this vision.
- Allow enough time for students to share their visions. If possible, invite community leaders to hear the final projects.

Personal Reflection:
- How can you take action to improve your community?
- What other areas of your life would you like to make a change? What action steps will you take? What do you expect the outcome to be?

Group Reflection:

- How can small acts make a big difference?
- Can people of all ages make a difference in their communities?
- How does making a difference feel?

Extended Learning:

Internet memes have the potential to go viral! Visit Project MASH and have students create and track an Internet meme about a change they would like to see in their community or in the world. Visit http://alpha.projectmash.org/experience/change-your-meme for more information.

Notes:

Grades 6-8: Confidence to Take Action Activities

Letter to the Editor

(ABOUT 50 MINUTES)

Common Core:
CCSS.ELA-LITERACY.W.6.1
Write arguments to support claims with clear reasons and relevant evidence.

21st Century Skills:
Communication, Media Literacy, Critical Thinking and Problem Solving

ISTE/NETS:
Communication and collaboration A, B

Research and information fluency C

Critical thinking, problem solving and decision making C

Digital citizenship A

Confidence to Take Action:
Confidence to Take Action can involve persuading others to take up a cause you believe in.

Objective:
Students will be able to write a persuasive editorial piece regarding a current event or relevant issue.

Materials:
Editorial pages from newspaper, magazines, or online.

Steps:

- Explain that one effective way to have your opinion and ideas heard is to write a letter to the editor. Many people read editorial pages of newspapers or magazines, and often a letter or e-mail to the editor will shine light on an important issue. In this activity, students will be asked to write letters to the editor about an issue that concerns them.

- Have students read a variety of editorials from online sources. Visit the *New York Times* student editorial contest site at http://nyti.ms/1tyLeyW. Ask: What are your thoughts on the editorials? Do you agree with them? What makes a good editorial?

- Inform your students that they are going to write a letter to the editor about an issue that concerns them that was brought up in a recent issue of the newspaper or magazine. First, students should find an article to form an opinion on or students can select a topic first and then choose the newspaper or magazine that best fits the topic.

- Compile the student letters into a classroom blog or forum.

- Have students read and respond to each other's editorials.

- Have students find e-mail addresses to the editor of the publications and mail them. Be sure to keep a watch for students' letters being published.

Personal Reflection:

- What was it like to voice your opinion?
- When do you voice your opinion at school?
- When do you voice your opinion in life? Give examples.
- Write a letter to your principal about an issue that matters to the class or you personally.

Group Reflection:

- Why do people read editorials?
- What constitutes a good editorial?
- Why is it important for students to voice their opinions?
- How do students have voice at school?

Extended Learning:

Have students voice their opinions about movies. Go to www.rottentomatoes.com. What constitutes a good review? Read several critic reviews and user reviews. Write a review on a movie you have recently watched in class or outside of school. How do you effectively voice your opinion online or in other forums?

Notes:
_____
_____
_____
_____
_____
_____
_____
_____

Grades 3-5: Confidence to Take Action Activities

Confidence Commercials

(ABOUT 40 MINUTES)

Common Core:
CCSS.ELA-LITERACY.W.3-5.6
With some guidance and support from adults, use technology, including the Internet, to produce and publish writing as well as to interact and collaborate with others.

CCSS.ELA-LITERACY.SL.3-5.5
Add audio recordings and visual displays to presentations when appropriate to enhance the development of main ideas or themes.

21st Century Skills:
Creativity and Innovation, ICT Literacy, Media Literacy, Communication, Collaboration

ISTE/NETS:
Communication and collaboration A, B, D

Creativity and innovation A, B

Digital citizenship A, B, C, D

Technology operations and concepts A, B, C, D

Confidence to Take Action:
Confidence to Take Action is about believing in yourself and your abilities. This activity helps build confidence through hearing from friends about their positive attributes.

Objective:
Students will be able to create a commercial about a classmate that highlights the partner's positive attributes.

Materials:
Devices or computer with iMovie or moviemaker.

Steps:

- Warm-up discussion: What does it mean to be confident? What are you confident about?
- Spend a few minutes discussing some familiar commercials with the class.
- Have students create a list of things they feel confident about.
- Divide the class into pairs. Ask each partner to compose a commercial about the other student to build their confidence and highlight their skills and strengths. Students might have to spend some time talking to get to know each other better.
- Next, have students write and brainstorm their ideas about the theme and story in their commercial and how it connects to a product.
- Some commercial ideas might include characteristics such as a good friend, great athlete, talented musician, smart student. Some commercials tell a story or have a theme.
- Encourage students to be creative. Using iMovie or moviemaker, students will record, edit, and add special effects to their commercials.
- Allow students to present their commercials. You may show commercials all at once or show them for a quick break during other lessons.

Personal Reflection:

- Why is it important to believe in yourself and your abilities?
- What abilities do you have that you are proud of?

Group Reflection:

- Did you notice all of us have a lot of potential?
- Should we use our skills to be the best people we can be? Why?
- How can we use our skills to make a difference? Give examples.

Extended Learning:

Students can create a Pinterest board of pictures that represent their different skills and talents. Students can also pin quotes about self-confidence, self-esteem, and motivational quotes.

Notes:
_____
_____
_____
_____
_____
_____
_____
_____
_____
_____
_____
_____

Grades 3-5: Confidence to Take Action Activities

Selfie-Confidence

(ABOUT 20–30 MINUTES)

Common Core:
CCSS.ELA-LITERACY.SL.3-5.1
Engage effectively in a range of collaborative discussions (one-on-one, in groups, and teacher-led) with diverse partners on *grade 3-5 topics and texts*, building on others' ideas and expressing their own clearly.

21st Century Skills:
Creativity and Innovation, Collaboration, Social and Cross-Cultural Interaction

ISTE/NETS:
Creativity and innovation B
Communication and collaboration D
Research and information fluency B

Confidence to Take Action:
Confidence to Take Action is about believing in yourself and your abilities and celebrating other students' abilities. Students of all ages should be proud of who they are and express why they are proud of other students too.

Objective:
Students will be able to create a reflection of their own self-confidence.

Materials:
Whiteboard; digital camera.

Steps:
- Warm-up discussion: What does it mean to be self-confident? What does it mean to be proud of who you are? What are you confident about? How can you support other students to be confident in their abilities?
- Explain to students that they are going to participate in an exercise in building self-confidence.
- Allow students to research different compliments online and create vocabulary words.
- Next, have one student stand in front of a whiteboard while others write a positive phrase about them with an arrow pointing to them (e.g., funny, brightens my day, great listener, positive). Take each student's "selfie" and give it to the student.

Personal Reflection:
- What are you self-confident about?
- What does it feel like to have other students believe in you?

Group Reflection:

How can you help other students believe in themselves?

Discuss the following statements:

- To improve Confidence to Take Action for myself, I will _____.
- To improve Confidence to Take Action for other students, I will _____.
- To improve Confidence to Take Action for everyone, we will _____.

Extended Learning:

Ask: Why is it important to be confident about pursuing your dreams? What are your dreams? Learn about different careers at http://kids.usa.gov/jobs/. Pick several different careers to learn about. What skills are needed for that job? What career do you think you would enjoy and be successful at? Explain.

Students will create their own selfie-confidence posts. Using PicCollage, have students take a pictures of themselves. Then add text! Students can type characteristics that they have that they are proud of. Change the color and font to make it a work of art.

Notes:

_____
_____
_____
_____
_____
_____
_____
_____

Grades 3-5: Confidence to Take Action Activities

Students Sharing Skills

(ABOUT 30–40 MINUTES)

Common Core:
CCSS.ELA-LITERACY.W.3.1
Write opinion pieces on topics or texts, supporting a point of view with reasons.

21st Century Skills:
Creativity and Innovation, Collaboration

ISTE/NETS:
Creativity and innovation B

Communication and collaboration A, B

Digital citizenship B

Confidence to Take Action:

Confidence to Take Action is about being confident in your abilities and then doing something with your confidence. This activity encourages students to share their experiences with younger students.

Objective:

Students will be able to formulate advice to younger students to prepare for the upcoming year.

Materials:

Technology for writing a blog (e.g., Blogster) or materials to write letters.

Steps:

- Warm-up discussion: What advice do you wish you received before the start of the school year? How can we help younger students prepare for this grade? What is an area where you feel confident?
- Ask students to write a typed letter to younger students or write a blog post for younger students about how to be successful in third, fourth, or fifth grade. Students should share their experiences in their current grade, what they learned, what skills they needed, and how they were successful in different areas of school.
- Student can include information about academics, social experiences, and extracurricular activities. Students may write funny stories, how to get involved with a sport, and what games are fun to play at recess. Students can add pictures or videos to enhance their writing.

Personal Reflection:

- How can confidence be built by helping others?
- Write a story about a time when you helped someone else and it helped build your own confidence.

Group Reflection:

- How can confidence be built by helping others?
- Brainstorm a list of ways to help others.
- What is it like to share what we know with others?
- If you have strong skills in one area, should you help others that struggle in this skill?

Extended Learning:

Using the app Chatterpix Kids, students should take a picture of someone or something (e.g., dog, soccer ball, stuffed animal, class pet). Students should draw a line for a mouth, and then record their voice. Students should give advice about a skill that they have. For example, if a student is a good soccer player, he can explain how to score a goal. The Chatterpix Kids creations should be shared with the class or with the students reading the letters in the younger grades.

Source: Courtesy of Chatterpix Kids.

Notes:

_____
_____
_____
_____
_____
_____
_____
_____
_____

Grades K-2: Confidence to Take Action Activities

Selfie-Confidence 2.0

(ABOUT 20–30 MINUTES)

Common Core:
CCSS.ELA-LITERACY.SL.K-2.1 Engage effectively in a range of collaborative discussions (one-on-one, in groups, and teacher-led) with diverse partners on *grade K-2 topics and texts*, building on others' ideas and expressing their own clearly.

CCSS.ELA-LITERACY.W.K-2.6 With guidance and support from adults, explore a variety of digital tools to produce and publish writing, including in collaboration with peers.

21st Century Skills:
Creativity and Innovation, Collaboration, Social and Cross-Cultural Interaction

ISTE/NETS:
Creativity and innovation B
Communication and collaboration D
Research and information fluency B
Digital citizenship B
Technology operations and concepts A, B, C, D

Confidence to Take Action:

Confidence to Take Action is about believing in yourself and abilities. This activity helps students understand more about themselves.

Objective:

Students will create a visual representation of what traits and skills they are proud of.

Materials:

PicCollage app; devices.

Steps:

What does it mean to be confident? What are you confident about?

- As a class, brainstorm and list some traits to be proud of.
- Tell students that they will celebrate what they are proud of.
- Students will take a picture of themself or have someone take a picture of them.
- Next, open up PicCollage app. Click start a new collage. Have students add the photo. Next, allow students to add text. Students will type words that describe them and things they are confident in: funny, kind, loving, helpful, fast runner, math, reading, silly, brother. Assist students as needed.

- Save the pictures and e-mail to students or parents to keep! With permission, post on classroom website. Display pictures as computer background or screen saver slideshow.
- Teachers should create one, too, and show students!

Personal Reflection:

Complete the following statements:

- I am getting better at _____.
- I am good at _____.
- I am great at _____.
- I work really hard at _____.
- I'm a good friend because _____.
- I love doing _____.
- I like when other students _____.
- I enjoy helping others to _____.
- I would love to learn how to _____.
- Someday I would like to _____.

Group Reflection:

- Did you notice each of us has so much potential?
- Take a look at all these reasons to be confident! Why is it important to believe in yourself and your abilities?
- How can we use our skills to make a difference?

Source: Photo by Julie Hellerstein.

Extended Learning:

Have students create a graphic organizer or web by using the Popplet app. In the center, students should write a circle that says things they are confident about. Next, students can write sentences and pictures of what they like. Students should add on to this web throughout the year as they build more skills and confidence.

Access other self-esteem activities and discussion questions from kidshealth.org and http://classroom.kidshealth.org/classroom/prekto2/personal/growing/self_esteem.pdf.

Notes:

_____

_____

Grades K-2: Confidence to Take Action Activities

Confident to Change

(ABOUT 20–30 MINUTES)

Common Core:
CCSS.ELA-LITERACY.W.K-2.7
Participate in shared research and writing projects

21st Century Skills:
Critical Thinking and Problem Solving, Creativity and Innovation, Communication, Collaboration

ISTE/NETS:
Creativity and innovation A

Research and information fluency A, B, C

Communication and collaboration B, D

Confidence to Take Action:

Confidence to Take Action is about feeling empowered to make a difference.

Objective:

Students will be able to solve a problem or issue using a new solution.

Materials:

Access to Internet; Popplet or concept mapping tool.

Steps:

- Select a relevant school issue, for example, littering. Students can create a *K-W-L* chart about this topic. Allow students to use technology to acquire more background knowledge about the topic.
- Next, present students with how this issue impacts the school. For example, many kids drop trash at the playground. The playground does not feel very clean or safe because there is trash everywhere. Ask students to problem solve: What could you do to make sure kids put trash in the trashcan and not on the playground?
- Have students brainstorm and record ideas to create a new solution or solve the issue.
- Use Popplet or another concept map, to guide students' brainstorming.
- Allow students to test their solution to the school problem.

Personal Reflection:

- What is it like to gather and organize ideas about a topic?
- What does it feel like to know that you can make a difference?
- What can you do to help with the project?
- What are some other small things you can do every day to make a difference?

Group Reflection:

- Why is it important to collaborate and share ideas?
- Did we create a new solution to the problem? Do you think the solution will work?
- What will we need to do to carry out our plan?
- What are some small things students can do every day?
- Why is it important to be confident in knowing you can make a difference?

Extended Learning:

Students should write words of wisdom for new students. Ask: What does it mean to share your wisdom with others? Collect students' thoughts and make a digital poster like a Thinglink to share each student's ideas. Thinglink can share webpages, videos, and other pictures. Allow students to help build it. Another option is to create a Stormboard. Allow students to post their own ideas and comment. Ask: Why is it important to share your knowledge and to help others? Does helping others build your confidence? Why?

Notes:
___
___
___
___
___
___
___
___

Grades K-2: Confidence to Take Action Activities

Career Quest

(ABOUT 30–50 MINUTES)

Common Core:
CCSS.ELA-LITERACY.W.K-2.7 Participate in shared research and writing projects.

CCSS.ELA-LITERACY.SL.K-2.1 Participate in collaborative conversations with diverse partners about *K-2 topics and texts* with peers and adults in small and larger groups.

21st Century Skills:
Communication, Critical Thinking and Problem Solving, Information Literacy, Initiative and Self-Direction

ISTE/NETS:
Digital citizenship B, C, D

Technology operations and concepts A

Research and information fluency A

Communication and collaboration B, D

Confidence to Take Action:

Confidence to Take Action is about exploring your skills, interests, and future opportunities.

Objective:

Students will be able to research a potential career, identify responsibilities and skills of the career, and evaluate what skills they have now that relate to this position.

Materials:

Internet access; student presentation materials may vary.

Steps:

- Ask students to list examples of careers. Ask guiding questions so students recall a number of careers. Who do you call when your dog is sick? Who makes sure the school is safe and clean? Who answers the phone and organizes important papers for the principal? Who do you see when you are sick?
- Students should now list some of the things they are interested in and like to do. Allow students to share ideas. Ask the class if they can think of any careers that go with that idea. For example, if a student says she likes dolphins, ask students to think of careers where you would work with dolphins.
- From this discussion, invite students to research a career of their choice and answer the following questions.
    - What would a day in the life of a _____ be like?
    - What would your responsibilities be? What would you do at work?
    - What skills would you need to have?
    - Do you have any of these skills today?
    - What skills will you want to work on so you can be successful in this career someday?

- Students should present their findings to the class. When students present, have them bring in a prop, dress up in a costume, or have a visual aide that helps other students understand the job better.

Personal Reflection:

- Draw a picture of what you imagine your future to look like. What could you do now to get there someday?
- Go to http://ibelieveinme.org/onlineColoring2.html. Select a career from the online coloring book and color it in! Click through different jobs to get a sense of what careers are out there.

Group Reflection:

- Can developing skills now help you for your future dreams?
- What can you do right now in the present?
- What are you confident about?
- Did you notice how a variety of careers are represented in our class?
- Do you think all students should pursue the same career? Why or why not?
- Why is it good for a community to have people who have different skills, interests, and backgrounds?

Extended Learning:

Students should explore their interests and learn about different careers through a simulation called Paws in Jobland at http://paws.bridges.com/cfnc1.htm. Invite students to take the JobFinder quiz. Based on quiz results, certain buildings in the virtual city will be illuminated. Students can click on these buildings and explore different jobs through watching short videos.

Notes:
_____
_____
_____
_____
_____

APPENDIX A

Common Core State Standards, Grades K–8

	BELONGING			HEROES			SENSE OF ACCOMPLISHMENT			FUN & EXCITEMENT			CURIOSITY & CREATIVITY			SPIRIT OF ADVENTURE			LEADERSHIP & RESPONSIBILITY			CONFIDENCE TO TAKE ACTION		
	6-8	3-5	K-2	6-8	3-5	K-2	6-8	3-5	K-2	6-8	3-5	K-2	6-8	3-5	K-2	6-8	3-5	K-2	6-8	3-5	K-2	6-8	3-5	K-2
CCSS.ELA—LITERACY.CCRA.W.3																								
CCSS.ELA—LITERACY.SL.6.1	X						X			X			X						X			X		
CCSS.ELA—LITERACY.SL.7.1	X						X			X			X						X			X		
CCSS.ELA—LITERACY.SL.8.1	X						X						X						X			X		
CCSS.ELA—LITERACY.W.6.6	X						X																	
CCSS.ELA—LITERACY.W.7.6	X																							
CCSS.ELA—LITERACY.W.8.6	X																							
CCSS.ELA—LITERACY.CCRA.W 4	X			X	X		X																	
CCSS.ELA—LITERACY.CCRA.W 6	X			X												X								
CCSS.ELA—LITERACY.RI.7.1				X																				
CCSS.ELA—LITERACY.CCRA.R.7				X			X																	
CCSS.ELA—LITERACY.W.6.2																			X					
CCSS.ELA—LITERACY.W.6.4							X									X								

	BELONGING			HEROES			SENSE OF ACCOMPLISHMENT			FUN & EXCITEMENT			CURIOSITY & CREATIVITY			SPIRIT OF ADVENTURE			LEADERSHIP & RESPONSIBILITY			CONFIDENCE TO TAKE ACTION		
	6-8	3-5	K-2	6-8	3-5	K-2	6-8	3-5	K-2	6-8	3-5	K-2	6-8	3-5	K-2	6-8	3-5	K-2	6-8	3-5	K-2	6-8	3-5	K-2
CCSS.ELA—LITERACY.SL.8.4										X						X			X					
CCSS.ELA—LITERACY.W.HST.7													X									X		
CCSS.ELA—LITERACY.W.6-8.10													X									X		
CCSS.ELA—LITERACY.SL.7.4																X			X					
CCSS.ELA—LITERACY.SL.6-8.5																X								
CCSS.ELA—LITERACY.W.6-8.2																X			X					
CCSS.ELA—LITERACY.W.6-8.3	X																							
CCSS.ELA—LITERACY.SL 4	X							X																
CCSS.ELA—LITERACY.SL.4.4	X																							
CCSS.ELA—LITERACY.CCRA.SL.5	X																							
CCSS.ELA—LITERACY.SL.4.1	X							X			X						X							
CCSS.ELA—LITERACY.W.4.4	X							X																
CCSS.ELA—LITERACY.SL.K-2.1			X									X						X						X
CCSS.ELA—LITERACY.RL.K.1			X						X									X						
CCSS.ELA—LITERACY.RL.K.2			X						X									X						
CCSS.ELA—LITERACY.RL.K.3			X																					
CCSS.ELA—LITERACY.RL.K.10			X						X															

(Continued)

(Continued)

	BELONGING			HEROES			SENSE OF ACCOMPLISHMENT			FUN & EXCITEMENT			CURIOSITY & CREATIVITY			SPIRIT OF ADVENTURE			LEADERSHIP & RESPONSIBILITY			CONFIDENCE TO TAKE ACTION		
	6-8	3-5	K-2	6-8	3-5	K-2	6-8	3-5	K-2	6-8	3-5	K-2	6-8	3-5	K-2	6-8	3-5	K-2	6-8	3-5	K-2	6-8	3-5	K-2
CCSS.ELA–LITERACY.RL.1.2			X						X									X						
CCSS.ELA–LITERACY.RL.1.3			X						X			X						X						
CCSS.ELA–LITERACY.RL.2.2			X															X						
CCSS.ELA–LITERACY.L.4.2.D					X																			
CCSS.ELA–LITERACY 4.4.C					X																			
CCSS.ELA–LITERACY.RI.4.9					X																			
CCSS.ELA–LITERACY.RI.4.6					X	X																		
CCSS.ELA–LITERACY.RI.1.1						X																		
CCSS.ELA–LITERACY.RI.1.2						X																		
CCSS.ELA–LITERACY.RI.1.3						X																		
CCSS.ELA–LITERACY.W.1.3						X									X									
CCSS.ELA–LITERACY.W.4.2								X																
CCSS.ELA–LITERACY.W.4.2 D								X																
CCSS.ELA–LITERACY.W.4.3 D								X									X							
CCSS.ELA–LITERACY.W.4.10								X																
CCSS.ELA–LITERACY.RL.2.1									X															
CCSS.ELA–LITERACY.RL.2.2									X															
CCSS.ELA–LITERACY.RL.2.3									X			X												

	BELONGING			HEROES			SENSE OF ACCOMPLISHMENT			FUN & EXCITEMENT			CURIOSITY & CREATIVITY			SPIRIT OF ADVENTURE			LEADERSHIP & RESPONSIBILITY			CONFIDENCE TO TAKE ACTION		
	6-8	3-5	K-2	6-8	3-5	K-2	6-8	3-5	K-2	6-8	3-5	K-2	6-8	3-5	K-2	6-8	3-5	K-2	6-8	3-5	K-2	6-8	3-5	K-2
CCSS.ELA—LITERACY.SL.3.1											X						X							
CCSS.ELA—LITERACY.SL 5.1											X						X							
CCSS.ELA—LITERACY.SL.4.1.D											X													
CCSS.ELA—LITERACY.SL.4.1.C											X													
CCSS.ELA—LITERACY.SL.1.1.B												X												
CCSS.ELA—LITERACY.W.K.2												X												
CCSS.ELA—LITERACY.RF.K.2.A												X												X
CCSS.ELA—LITERACY.W.K-2.6												X												
CCSS.ELA—LITERACY.W.3-5.7														X										
CCSS.ELA—LITERACY.W.5.9														X										
CCSS.ELA—LITERACY.W.3-5.7														X										
CCSS.ELA—LITERACY.SL 3-5.1														X	X					X			X	
CCSS.ELA—LITERACY.W.K.3															X								X	
CCSS.ELA—LITERACY.W.2.3															X									
CCSS.ELA—LITERACY.W.K.8															X									
CCSS.ELA—LITERACY.W.1.8															X									
CCSS.ELA—LITERACY.W.2.8															X									
CCSS.ELA—LITERACY.RF.1-2.4 C															X									
CCSS.ELA—LITERACY.L.K-2.1															X									

(Continued)

(Continued)

	BELONGING			HEROES			SENSE OF ACCOMPLISHMENT			FUN & EXCITEMENT			CURIOSITY & CREATIVITY			SPIRIT OF ADVENTURE			LEADERSHIP & RESPONSIBILITY			CONFIDENCE TO TAKE ACTION		
	6-8	3-5	K-2	6-8	3-5	K-2	6-8	3-5	K-2	6-8	3-5	K-2	6-8	3-5	K-2	6-8	3-5	K-2	6-8	3-5	K-2	6-8	3-5	K-2
CCSS.ELA–LITERACY.W.4.10																	X			X				
CCSS.ELA–LITERACY.W.5.10																	X			X				
CCSS.ELA–LITERACY.RL.2.1																		X						
CCSS.ELA–LITERACY.RL.2.3																		X						
CCSS.ELA–LITERACY.W.1.2																		X						
CCSS.ELA–LITERACY.W.1.8																		X						
CCSS.ELA–LITERACY.W.3-5.1																				X				
CCSS.ELA–LITERACY.W.3-5.4																				X				
CCSS.ELA–LITERACY.SL.K-2.1																					X			
CCSS.ELA–LITERACY.SL.2.5																					X			
CCSS.ELA–LITERACY.SL.2.4																					X			
CCSS.MATH–CONTENT.2.MD.C.8																					X			
CCSS.ELA–LITERACY.W.K.1																					X			
CCSS.ELA–LITERACY.W.1.1																					X			
CCSS.ELA–LITERACY.W.2.1																					X			
CCSS.ELA–LITERACY.W.3-5.6																							X	
CCSS.ELA–LITERACY.SL.3-5.5																							X	
CCSS.ELA–LITERACY.W.K-2.7																								X

APPENDIX B

Partnership for 21st Century Skills, Grades K–8

	BELONGING			HEROES			SENSE OF ACCOMPLISHMENT			FUN & EXCITEMENT			CURIOSITY & CREATIVITY			SPIRIT OF ADVENTURE			LEADERSHIP & RESPONSIBILITY			CONFIDENCE TO TAKE ACTION		
	6-8	3-5	K-2	6-8	3-5	K-2	6-8	3-5	K-2	6-8	3-5	K-2	6-8	3-5	K-2	6-8	3-5	K-2	6-8	3-5	K-2	6-8	3-5	K-2
Critical Thinking and Problem Solving	X	X			X	X	X		X	X	X	X	X	X					X	X	X	X		X
Creativity and Innovation	X		X	X	X	X	X	X		X	X	X	X	X	X	X	X	X		X		X	X	X
Communication	X	X	X	X	X	X	X	X	X	X	X	X				X	X	X	X		X	X	X	X
Collaboration	X	X	X	X	X	X	X	X	X	X	X	X	X	X		X	X	X	X	X		X	X	X
Information Literacy								X		X					X									X
Media Literacy							X			X		X	X	X		X	X		X		X	X	X	
ICT Literacy	X	X	X						X					X				X		X			X	
Flexibility and Adaptability											X			X			X	X						
Initiative and Self-Direction		X			X		X	X	X					X		X	X	X		X	X			X
Social and Cross-Cultural Interaction	X	X	X		X			X										X	X	X				X
Productivity and Accountability													X	X		X		X						
Leadership and Responsibility		X	X	X	X	X	X	X											X	X	X		X	X

189

APPENDIX C

ISTE Standards, Grades K–8

	BELONGING			HEROES			SENSE OF ACCOMPLISHMENT			FUN & EXCITEMENT			CURIOSITY & CREATIVITY			SPIRIT OF ADVENTURE			LEADERSHIP & RESPONSIBILITY			CONFIDENCE TO TAKE ACTION		
	6-8	3-5	K-2	6-8	3-5	K-2	6-8	3-5	K-2	6-8	3-5	K-2	6-8	3-5	K-2	6-8	3-5	K-2	6-8	3-5	K-2	6-8	3-5	K-2
1. Creativity and Innovation A	X	X		X	X	X		X		X	X	X	X	X	X	X	X	X				X	X	X
1. Creativity and Innovation B	X			X	X	X	X	X	X	X	X	X	X	X		X	X	X				X	X	X
1. Creativity and Innovation C	X		X		X									X				X				X		
1. Creativity and Innovation D	X									X				X	X						X	X		
2. Communication and Collaboration A	X		X	X	X	X		X		X		X	X	X										
2. Communication and Collaboration B	X	X		X			X	X	X	X		X				X	X					X	X	X
2. Communication and Collaboration C	X		X					X																
2. Communication and Collaboration D	X			X			X	X		X	X		X		X		X		X			X	X	X
3. Research and Information Fluency A	X	X		X		X								X		X								X
3. Research and Information Fluency B	X			X	X	X		X					X	X					X	X	X	X	X	X
3. Research and Information Fluency C	X				X	X							X	X					X		X			X
3. Research and Information Fluency D	X												X	X	X						X			

190

	BELONGING			HEROES			SENSE OF ACCOMPLISHMENT			FUN & EXCITEMENT			CURIOSITY & CREATIVITY			SPIRIT OF ADVENTURE			LEADERSHIP & RESPONSIBILITY			CONFIDENCE TO TAKE ACTION		
	6-8	3-5	K-2	6-8	3-5	K-2	6-8	3-5	K-2	6-8	3-5	K-2	6-8	3-5	K-2	6-8	3-5	K-2	6-8	3-5	K-2	6-8	3-5	K-2
4. Critical Thinking, Problem Solving and Decision Making B										X			X	X						X	X			
4. Critical Thinking, Problem Solving and Decision Making C									X	X			X	X	X				X					
4. Critical Thinking, Problem Solving and Decision Making D					X	X			X	X		X	X	X					X	X				
5. Digital Citizenship A	X																							
5. Digital Citizenship B	X	X		X	X			X	X	X						X		X		X	X	X	X	X
5. Digital Citizenship C															X			X					X	X
5. Digital Citizenship D								X										X		X	X		X	X
6. Technology Operations and Concepts A	X				X			X	X	X	X				X			X		X	X		X	X
6. Technology Operations and Concepts B		X							X	X								X		X	X		X	X
6. Technology Operations and Concepts C											X									X	X		X	X
6. Technology Operations and Concepts D	X								X										X	X	X		X	X

Index

Achievement, student. *See* Confidence to take action; Sense of accomplishment
Acting It Out activity, 94–95
Addressing Assumption activity, 149–151
Adventure. *See* Spirit of adventure
Adventure Action Cards activity, 128–239
Adventure Advice activity, 122–123
Alike and Different activity, 20–21
All About Me Cloud and Class Cloud activity, 7–8
Appy Hour activity, 80–81
Aspirations
   Aspirations Framework, xiii
   Aspirations Profile, xi–xii, xii (figure)
   definition of, xi
   dynamic continuum of, xii–xiii
Award Show activity, 62–64

Belonging
   characteristics of, 1–2
   definition of, 1, xiv
   grades K–2 activities, 20–26
   grades 6–8 activities, 3–10
   grades 3–5 activities, 11–19
Belong-Meme activity, 9–10
Best Music Apps for Kids, 85
Billings, Josh, 69
Buckets activity, 22–24
Build a Band activity, 84–85
Bull's Eye activity, 130–131

Career Quest activity, 182–183
Change the World in 5 Minutes—Everyday at School, 73
Chatterpix Kids, 177
Citizen Action Plan activity, 72–73
Citizenship, 51, 72–73
Class dojo, 61
Class Mascot activity, 14–16
CNN Heroes website, 30
Collaboration, student. *See* Belonging
Common Core State Standards, xi, xv
   grades K–2 Belonging activities and, 20 (box), 22 (box), 25 (box)

grades K–2 Confidence to Take Action activities and, 178 (box), 180 (box), 182 (box)
grades K–2 Curiosity & Creativity activities and, 112 (box), 114 (box), 116 (box)
grades K–2 Fun & Excitement activities and, 91 (box), 94 (box), 96 (box)
grades K–2 Heroes activities and, 43 (box), 45 (box), 48 (box)
grades K–2 Leadership & Responsibility activities and, 156 (box), 158 (box), 161 (box)
grades K–2 Sense of Accomplishment activities and, 70 (box), 72 (box), 74 (box)
grades K–2 Spirit of Adventure activities and, 132 (box), 134 (box), 136 (box)
grades 6–8 Belonging activities and, 3 (box), 7 (box), 9 (box)
grades 6–8 Confidence to Take Action activities and, 165 (box), 168 (box), 170 (box)
grades 6–8 Curiosity & Creativity activities and, 100 (box), 102 (box), 104 (box)
grades 6–8 Fun & Excitement activities and, 78 (box), 80 (box), 82 (box)
grades 6–8 Heroes activities and, 29 (box), 31 (box), 33 (box)
grades 6–8 Leadership & Responsibility activities and, 140 (box), 142 (box), 144 (box)
grades 6–8 Sense of Accomplishment activities and, 53 (box), 55 (box), 59 (box)
grades 6–8 Spirit of Adventure activities and, 120 (box), 122 (box), 124 (box)
grades 3–5 Belonging activities and, 11 (box), 14 (box), 17 (box)
grades 3–5 Confidence to Take Action activities and, 172 (box), 174 (box), 176 (box)

grades 3–5 Curiosity & Creativity activities and, 106 (box), 108 (box), 110 (box)
grades 3–5 Fun & Excitement activities and, 84 (box), 86 (box), 88 (box)
grades 3–5 Heroes activities and, 35–36, 37 (box), 39 (box)
grades 3–5 Leadership & Responsibility activities and, 147 (box), 149 (box), 152 (box)
grades 3–5 Sense of Accomplishment activities and, 62 (box), 65 (box), 68 (box)
grades 3–5 Spirit of Adventure activities and, 126 (box), 128 (box), 130 (box)
summary of activities and, 184–188 (table)
Confidence Commercials activity, 172–173
Confidence to take action
   characteristics in, xv
   grades K–2 activities, 178–183
   grades 6–8 activities, 165–171
   grades 3–5 activities, 172–177
Confident to Change activity, 180–181
Congratulations Card activity, 74–75
Coyle, Carmela, 43
Creativity. *See* Curiosity and creativity
Critical thinking, 39–40 48–49, 80–83, 100–113
Cultural Connections activity, 25–26
Curiosity and creativity
   characteristics of, 98–99, xiv
   grades K–2 activities, 112–117
   grades 6–8 activities, 100–105
   grades 3–5 activities, 106–111
The Curiosity Convention activity, 102–103

Debate, 140–141
Dibu's Monster Maker app, 11, 13
Digital Story Telling activity, 96–97
Discovery Education lesson plans, 151
Discuss and Decide activity, 152–155
Diversity, student, 25–26

Do Super Heroes Have Teddy Bears? (Coyle), 43
Drawing Dictations activity, 142–143

Edison, Thomas, 68
Edmodo website, 8
Educreations Interactive Whiteboard app, 113
8 Conditions That Make a Difference™, overview of, xiv–xv
Einstein, Albert, 103
Engagement, xiii
   See also Curiosity and creativity; Fun and excitement in school; Spirit of adventure
Extreme Community Makeover activity, 168–169

Famous Failures (video), 53, 54
Field trips, 118
For the Birds (video), 49
From Failing You Learn, Keep Moving Forward (video clip), 127
Fun and excitement in school
   grades K–2 activities, 91–97
   grades 6–8 activities, 78–83
   grades 3–5 activities, 84–90
   student engagement and, 76–77, xiv
   types of, 76–77

GarageBand app, 85
Genius Gallery activity, 106–107
Genius Hour (video), 106
Goals, student, 55–56, 67, 69–70, 124–125
   See also Sense of accomplishment
Google Nexus TV commercials, 120
Grades K–2 Belonging activities
   Alike and Different, 20–21
   Buckets, 22–24
   Cultural Connections, 25–26
Grades K–2 Confidence to Take Action activities
   Career Quest, 182–183
   Confident to Change, 180–181
   Selfie-Confidence 2.0, 178–179
Grades K–2 Curiosity & Creativity activities
   Mad Libs, 116–117
   Surroundings Scavenger Hunt, 114–115
   What's in the Bag?, 112–113
Grades K–2 Fun & Excitement activities
   Acting It Out, 94–95
   Digital Story Telling, 96–97
   Scenarios, 91–93
Grades K–2 Heroes activities
   Hall of Fame, 45–47

   My Everyday Super Hero Cartoon, 43–44
   We Can Be Heroes-Me and You, 48–50
Grades K–2 Leadership & Responsibility activities
   Listening Blocks, 156–157
   Opportunity for Opinions, 161–162
   What Do You Think?, 158–160
Grades K–2 Sense of Accomplishment activities
   Citizen Action Plan, 72–73
   Congratulations Card, 74–75
   I Think I Can, 70–71
Grades K–2 Spirit of Adventure activities
   Hands-On Goals, 136–137
   Oh, the Places You'll Go, 134–135
   Skills Within Reach, 132–133
Grades 6–8 Belonging activities, 168–169
   All About Me Cloud and Class Cloud, 7–8
   Belong-Meme, 9–10
   Pick a Number, 3–6
Grades 6–8 Confidence to Take Action activities
   Extreme Community Makeover, 168–169
   Letter to the Editor, 170–171
   Time Capsule, 165–167
Grades 6–8 Curiosity & Creativity activities
   The Curiosity Convention, 102–103
   Marshmallow Challenge, 104–105
   Quick Question, 100–101
Grades 6–8 Fun & Excitement activities
   Appy Hour, 80–81
   Heads Up!, 78–79
   Un-Bored Games, 82–83
Grades 6–8 Heroes activities
   Gratitude, 33–34
   I Can Be a Hero Poem, 29–30
   Utilizing You!, 31–32
Grades 6–8 Leadership & Responsibility activities
   Drawing Dictations activity, 142–143
   Tag Team Debate, 140–141
   Values Auction, 144–146
Grades 6–8 Sense of Accomplishment activities
   Headline News, 59–61
   Marble Roll, 53–54
   Student Actions, 55–58
Grades 6–8 Spirit of Adventure activities
   Adventure Advice, 122–123
   Never Lose Sight of Your Goal, 124–125
   Student Speak, 120–121

Grades 3–5 Belonging activities
   Class Mascot, 14–16
   Personal Paper Doll, 11–13
   The Who Are You? Interview, 17 (box)
Grades 3–5 Confidence to Take Action activities
   Confidence Commercials, 172–173
   Selfie-Confidence, 174–175
   Students Sharing Skills, 176–177
Grades 3–5 Curiosity & Creativity activities
   Genius Gallery, 106–107
   Invention Convention, 110–111
   Mystery Picture, 108–109
Grades 3–5 Fun & Excitement activities
   Build a Band, 84–85
   Molding Minds, 86–87
   Story Starters, 88–90
Grades 3–5 Heroes activities
   Hero Traits, 35–36
   Historic Museum Exhibit, 37–38
   Telligami About Heroes, 39–42
Grades 3–5 Leadership & Responsibility activities
   Addressing Assumptions, 149–151
   Discuss and Decide, 152–155
   My Voice and Choice, 147–148
Grades 3–5 Sense of Accomplishment activities
   Award Show, 62–64
   How to . . . , 65–67
   Perseverance Phrase, 68–69
Grades 3–5 Spirit of Adventure activities
   Adventure Action Cards, 128–239
   Bull's Eye, 130–131
   Support Me Selfie, 126–127
Graphic organizers, 45, 91
Gratitude activity, 33–34
Guiding principles
   engagement, xiii
   purpose, xiii
   self-worth, xiii

Hall of Fame activity, 45–47
Hands-On Goals activity, 136–137
Have You Filled a Bucket Today? A Guide to Daily Happiness for Kids (McCloud), 22
Headline News activity, 59–61
Heads Up! activity, 78–79
Heads Up! app, 78–79
Heroes
   characteristics of, 27–28
   grades K–2 activities, 43–50
   grades 6–8 activities, 29–34, 31–32
   grades 3–5 activities, 35–42, 37–38
   types of, xiv

Heroes Young Wonder: Joshua Williams (video), 30
Hero Traits activity, 35–36
Historic Museum Exhibit activity, 37–38
How to . . . activity, 65–67
"How to Conduct an Interview," 18
How to Do the Cupid Shuffle Kids Hip Hop Moves (video), 65

I Can Be a Hero Poem activity, 29–30
International Society for Technology in Education (ISTE) standards, xi
   in grades K–2 Belonging activities, 20 (box), 23 (box), 26 (box)
   in grades K–2 Confidence to Take Action activities, 178 (box), 180 (box), 182 (box)
   in grades K–2 Curiosity & Creativity activities, 112 (box), 114 (box), 116 (box)
   in grades K–2 Fun & Excitement activities, 91 (box), 94 (box), 96 (box)
   in grades K–2 Heroes activities, 43 (box), 45 (box), 48 (box)
   in grades K–2 Leadership & Responsibility activities, 156 (box), 158 (box), 161 (box)
   in grades K–2 Sense of Accomplishment activities, 70 (box), 72 (box), 74 (box)
   in grades K–2 Spirit of Adventure activities, 132 (box), 135 (box), 136 (box)
   in grades 6–8 Belonging activities, 3 (box), 7 (box), 9 (box)
   in grades 6–8 Confidence to Take Action activities, 165 (box), 168 (box), 170 (box)
   in grades 6–8 Curiosity & Creativity activities, 100 (box), 102 (box), 104 (box)
   in grades 6–8 Fun & Excitement activities, 78 (box), 80 (box), 82 (box)
   in grades 6–8 Heroes activities, 29 (box), 31 (box), 33 (box)
   in grades 6–8 Leadership & Responsibility activities, 140 (box), 142 (box), 144 (box)
   in grades 6–8 Sense of Accomplishment activities, 53 (box), 55 (box), 60 (box)
   in grades 6–8 Spirit of Adventure activities, 120 (box), 122 (box), 124 (box)
   in grades 3–5 Belonging activities, 11 (box), 14 (box), 17 (box)
   in grades 3–5 Confidence to Take Action activities, 172 (box), 174 (box), 176 (box)
   in grades 3–5 Curiosity & Creativity activities, 106 (box), 108 (box), 110 (box)
   in grades 3–5 Fun & Excitement activities, 84 (box), 86 (box), 88 (box)
   in grades 3–5 Heroes activities, 35 (box), 37 (box), 39 (box)
   in grades 3–5 Leadership & Responsibility activities, 147 (box), 149 (box), 152 (box)
   in grades 3–5 Sense of Accomplishment activities, 62 (box), 65 (box), 68 (box)
   in grades 3–5 Spirit of Adventure activities, 126 (box), 128 (box), 130 (box)
   summary of activities and, 190–191 (table)
Internet. *See* Technology use
Invention Convention activity, 110–111
I Think I Can activity, 70–71

Keller, Helen, 118
Kid President's Pep Talk to Teachers and Students! (video), 107
Kostecki, Jenny Sue, 25
K-W-L charts, 31–32, 114, 165, 180–181

Leadership and responsibility
   decision making, 138–139, 152–155
   grades K–2 activities, 156–162
   grades 6–8 activities, 140–146
   grades 3–5 activities, 147–155
   real-world problems and, 138
   and sense of purpose, xiv
Legally Blonde 2 (film), 60
Letter to the Editor activity, 170–171
Listening Blocks activity, 156–157
The Little Engine That Could, 70
Loewen, Nancy, 72

Mad Libs activity, 116–117
Mad Libs app, 116–117
Maiers, Angela, 103, 107
Marble Roll activity, 53–54
Marshmallow Challenge activity, 104–105
McCloud, Carol, 22
Memes, 9–10, 22
Molding Minds activity, 86–87
Music, 84–85
My Everyday Super Hero Cartoon, 43–44
Mystery Picture activity, 108–109
Mystery Skype, 26
My Voice and Choice activity, 147–148
My Voice National Report, 10

Never Lose Sight of Your Goal activity, 124–125

Oh, the Places You'll Go! (Seuss), 134
Oh, the Place You'll Go activity, 134–135
One Step at a Time Goal Achieving Cartoon Doodle (video), 137
Online activities. *See* Technology use
Opportunity for Opinions activity, 161–162
Oral presentation activities, 11–13

Partnership for 21st Century Skills, xi, xv
   in grades K–2 Belonging activities, 20 (box), 23 (box), 26 (box)
   in grades K–2 Confidence to Take Action activities, 178 (box), 180 (box), 182 (box)
   in grades K–2 Curiosity & Creativity activities, 112 (box), 114 (box), 116 (box)
   in grades K–2 Fun & Excitement activities, 91 (box), 94 (box), 96 (box)
   in grades K–2 Heroes activities, 43 (box), 45 (box), 48 (box)
   in grades K–2 Leadership & Responsibility activities, 156 (box), 158 (box), 161 (box)
   in grades K–2 Sense of Accomplishment activities, 70 (box), 72 (box), 74 (box)
   in grades K–2 Spirit of Adventure activities, 132 (box), 135 (box), 136 (box)
   in grades 6–8 Belonging activities, 3 (box), 7 (box), 9 (box)
   in grades 6–8 Confidence to Take Action activities, 165 (box), 168 (box), 170 (box)
   in grades 6–8 Curiosity & Creativity activities, 100 (box), 102 (box), 104 (box)
   in grades 6–8 Fun & Excitement activities, 78 (box), 80 (box), 82 (box)
   in grades 6–8 Heroes activities, 29 (box), 31 (box), 33 (box)
   in grades 6–8 Leadership & Responsibility activities, 140 (box), 142 (box), 144 (box)
   in grades 6–8 Sense of Accomplishment activities, 53 (box), 55 (box), 60 (box)
   in grades 6–8 Spirit of Adventure activities, 120 (box), 122 (box), 124 (box)
   in grades 3–5 Belonging activities, 11 (box), 14 (box), 17 (box)
   in grades 3–5 Confidence to Take Action activities, 172 (box), 174 (box), 176 (box)

in grades 3–5 Curiosity & Creativity activities, 106 (box), 108 (box), 110 (box)
in grades 3–5 Fun & Excitement activities, 84 (box), 86 (box), 88 (box)
in grades 3–5 Heroes activities, 35 (box), 37 (box), 39 (box)
in grades 3–5 Leadership & Responsibility activities, 147 (box), 149 (box), 152 (box)
in grades 3–5 Sense of Accomplishment activities, 62 (box), 65 (box), 68 (box)
in grades 3–5 Spirit of Adventure activities, 126 (box), 128 (box), 130 (box)
summary of activities and, 189 (table)
Paws in Jobland, 183
Peer relationships. *See* Belonging
Perseverance Phrase activity, 68–69
Personal Paper Doll activity, 11–13
PicCollage app, 68, 69, 178–179
Pick a Number activity, 3–6
Pickle's Paper Dolls app, 11, 13
Pinterest, 123
Poetry activity, 29–30
The Poetry App, 29
Polished Girlz organization, 155
Poll Everywhere survey tool, 62
Popplet mind map, 101, 180–181
Project MASH, 169
Public speaking, 120–121
Purpose, xiii
See also Confidence to take action; Leadership and responsibility

Quaglia Institute for Student Aspirations (QISA), 99
Quick Question activity, 100–101
Quiz tools, 6

Raising Student Aspirations (Quaglia, Corso & Hellerstein), xiv

Red Stamp app, 75
Role models. *See* Heroes
Roosevelt, Franklin D., 68

Same, Same But Different (Kostecki), 25
Scenarios activity, 91–93
Selfie-Confidence activity, 174–175
Selfie-Confidence 2.0 activity, 178–179
Self-worth, 31, 31 (box), xiii
See also Belonging; Heroes; Sense of accomplishment
Sense of accomplishment
benefits of, 51–52
characteristics of, xiv
grades K–2 activities, 70–75
grades 6–8 activities, 53–61
grades 3–5 activities, 62–69
Service learning, 163
See also Confidence to take action
"7 Ways Kids Can Earn Money," 160
"Shark Tank" Young Entrepreneurs (video), 111
ShowMe app, 13, 37, 43–44, 137
Skills Within Reach activity, 132–133
Skype, 26
Social media. *See* Technology use
Socrative app, 149–150
Spirit of adventure
field trips, 118
grades K–2 activities, 132–137
grades 6–8 activities, 120–125
grades 3–5 activities, 126–131
student engagement and, 118–119, xiv
Story Starters activity, 88–90
Student achievement. *See* Sense of accomplishment
Student Actions activity, 55–58
Student Speak activity, 120–121
Students Sharing Skills activity, 176–177
Support Me Selfie activity, 126–127
Surroundings Scavenger Hunt activity, 114–115
Survey creator tools, 6

Tag Team Debate activity, 140–141
Teaching Tolerance website, 21
Technology use
apps learning activity, 80–81
class dojo, 61
concept maps, 180–181
digital citizenship, 167
digital media presentations, 13
digital story-telling, 96–97
Internet memes, 9–10
music apps, 85
photo-editing tools, 68, 69, 124–125
quiz and survey tools, 6, 62, 149–150
Skype, 26
social media, 8, 10, 61
word cloud generator, 7, 101
TEDTalks for Kids, 21
Telligami About Heroes activity, 39–42
Telligami app, 39–40
Time Capsule activity, 165–167
Timehop app, 167
Toontastic app, 96, 97
TouchCast app, 18
21st Century Skills. *See* Partnership for 21st Century Skills
Twitter. *See* Technology use

Un-Bored Games activity, 82–83
Utilizing YOU! activity, 31–32

Values Auction activity, 144–146

Wall, Alanna, 155
Webkinz World website, 16
We Can Be Heroes—Me and You, 48–50
We Live Here Too (Loewen), 72
What Do You Think? activity, 158–160
What's in the Bag? activity, 112–113
The Who Are You? Interview activity, 17–19
Word clouds, 7–10
Wordsalad app, 7–8, 100, 101
Writing prompts, 89–90

Helping educators make the greatest impact

CORWIN HAS ONE MISSION: to enhance education through intentional professional learning.

We build long-term relationships with our authors, educators, clients, and associations who partner with us to develop and continuously improve the best evidence-based practices that establish and support lifelong learning.